Teach JAZZ:
Alfred Jazz

Recommended
for Grades 3–6

Chop-Mon...

MW00997509

Jazz Language Tutor
for General Music Instruction

Jazz Handbook for Elementary General Music Teachers
with 2 CDs and Reproducible Worksheets

Margaret Fitzgerald • Kimberly McCord • Shelly Berg

Featured Recordings:
How High the Moon
Summertime
Take the "A" Train

Alfred

Contents

UNIT 3 SOUL OF JAZZ

PART 1 COOKING IN JAZZ

Jam Session: *Listen to the Rhythm Section; Sticky Situation Rhythm Section; Transferring to Instruments*
Concert Time: *Sticky Situation (Scatch-mo Station room set up); Cookin' with the Rhythm Section (worksheet); Jammin'/ Arrangement of Sticky Situation; Comparing Class Recording with Jazz Group on CD (worksheet)*
Sitting In: Dizzy Gillespie and Charlie Parker
Link to Jazz Masters: "Salt Peanuts," Dizzy Gillespie (Listening Map); "Now's the Time," Charlie Parker
Link to Literature: *Charlie Parker Played Be Bop* by Chris Raschka. Orchard Books.

PART 2 JAMMING IN JAZZ

Jam Session: *Hip Scat and Groove on Three Pitches; Hip Scat and Move on Three Pitches; Improvising on Three Pitches; Scattin' with the Rhythm Section*
Concert Time: *Feelin' Mighty Hip; Jammin' on Feelin' Mighty Hip; Comparing Two Versions of Feelin' Mighty Hip (worksheet)*
Sitting In: Miles Davis
Link to Jazz Masters: "Summertime," Miles Davis (Listening Questions)
Link to Literature: *Hip Cat* by Jonathan London, illustrated by Woodleigh Hubbard. Chronicle Books.
Link to Literature: *Lookin' for Bird in the Big City* by Robert Burleigh, illustrated by Marek Los. Silver Whistle/Harcourt, Inc.

PART 3 FREEDOM IN JAZZ

Jam Session: *Jazzy Chords; Movin' to Jazzy Chords; Scat Singing to the Changes; Making the Changes (movement)*
Concert Time: *Dogs and Cats! (Dogs and Cats room set up); Improvising to Dogs and Cats!*
Sitting In: Benny Goodman
Link to Jazz Masters: "Sing, Sing, Sing," Benny Goodman and His Orchestra
Link to Literature: *Once Upon a Time in Chicago* by Jonah Winter, pictures by Jeanette Winter. Hyperion.
Link to Literature: *The Sound that Jazz Makes* by Carole Boston Weatherford, illustrated by Eric Velasquez. Walker and Company.

Acknowledgments

Thank you to those educators who tested our activities and gave us feedback: Sarah Guterman, Lynn Orzelek, Vivian Murray, Ann Patterson and Akosua Addo, plus those who gave us specific suggestions including Greg Carroll, Mike Fitzgerald, Johanna Rayman and Pam McCord. Former student teachers are also acknowledged for their assistance: Marie Gisonni, Joel Peterazio, Mary Haijj and Jason Steinnagel.

Chop-Monster Jr. CD Track Listing

UNIT 1   RHYTHM OF JAZZ

PART 1: GROOVING IN JAZZ

CD 1

Track	Activity Name	Concept
CD1-Track 01	Swinging Jazz	Listening
CD1-Track 02	Marching	Movement
CD1-Track 03	That's Swing	Movement
CD1-Track 04	That's Jazz	Performance Model
CD1-Track 05	That's Jazz	Backing Track
CD1-Track 06	Jazzy Hands	Movement
CD1-Track 07	Jazzy Band	Performance
CD1-Track 07	Jazzy Ride	Performance

PART 2: RESPONDING IN JAZZ

CD1-Track 06	Chop-Monster Groove	Movement
CD1-Track 07	Jazz Name Game	Backing Track
CD1-Track 08	Louis Armstrong Call-and-Response	Backing Track
CD1-Track 09	Jazz-Ma-Tazz Complete (ABACADA)	Performance Model
CD1-Track 10	Jazz-Ma-Tazz (ABA and ADA)	Backing Track

PART 3: SWINGING IN JAZZ

CD1-Track 11	Doodle-Dah Groove	Backing Track
CD1-Track 12	Let's Swing (Part 1)	Performance Model
CD1-Track 13	Doodle-dah, doodle-dah, that's swing (Part 2)	Performance Model
CD1-Track 14	Keep it going, make it swing (Part 3)	Performance Model
CD1-Track 15	Doodle-Dah Round	Backing Track
CD1-Track 16	Recess Time, Yes!	Performance Model
CD1-Track 15	Recess Time, Yes!	Backing Track
CD1-Track 17	Jazz-Ma-Tazz Section C (Singers-Jazz, Players-Jazz)	Backing Track
CD1-Track 18	Jazz-Ma-Tazz Complete (ABACADA)	Backing Track
CD1-Track 19	Jazz Train	Performance Model
CD1-Track 20	Jazz Train	Backing Track
CD1-Track 21	**Take the "A" Train** (Strayhorn)	Listening Map

UNIT 2   HEART OF JAZZ

PART 1: COMMUNICATING IN JAZZ

Track	Activity Name	Concept
CD1-Track 01	Piano Conversations	Listening
CD1-Track 22	Jazzy Conversations (Aunt Nora)	Backing Track
CD1-Track 23	Breakfast / Lunch	Performance Model
CD1-Track 24	Breakfast / Lunch	Backing Track
CD1-Track 25	Dinner	Performance Model
CD1-Track 07	Dinner	Backing Track
CD1-Track 26	Poppity Pop Panic	Performance Model
CD1-Track 27	Poppity Pop Panic	Backing Track
CD1-Track 24	Mystery Word Game	Backing Track

PART 2: SCATTING IN JAZZ

CD1-Track 28	I'm Scattin' / Scat and Groove (one pitch, F)	Call-and-Response
CD1-Track 29	More Scat and Groove	Call-and-Response
CD1-Track 30	Improvise on One Pitch	Backing Track

CD 2

UNIT 3   SOUL OF JAZZ

All tracks composed by Shelly Berg, Margaret Fitzgerald and
Kimberly McCord unless otherwise noted.
All arrangements by Shelly Berg.

Introduction

Why Chop-Monster Jr?

Jazz. O.K., let's teach jazz. America's music. Why don't we look around to see just what is out there to help. Hmmmm, I'm no "jazzer" by any means, so it will have to be something that I can understand and relate to, something I am comfortable with. Here is the Blues Chord Pattern—that is something I know, and I can do on Orff instruments, too—even throw in a few recorders. We can use the pentatonic scale to improvise with, maybe even try out "C Jam Blues." Yes indeed, that will be fine. The kids will raise their hands when the chords change, then they can improvise over this Orff arrangement based on the Blues Chord Pattern.

Does this sound at all familiar? It does to me, because that is basically how I taught jazz for over 20 years. I was never quite satisfied with the quality of the improvisation that my students did in class. They heard the chord changes, seemed to be able to "feel" the beat—but when they soloed it was, what I refer to as, "bangin' on the pentatonic."

What was I doing wrong? I am a French horn player and classically trained pianist, so I did not have a lot of jazz experience myself…was I modeling poorly? I have to admit that whenever I played a solo, I was uncomfortable improvising. I never felt that I could converse in the language of jazz. I had a lot of great listening examples, what was the problem?

The problem, as Kim McCord and I found out after a great deal of research and reflection, was that we weren't teaching our students to play jazz in a developmentally appropriate way. They didn't have the basic building blocks of experiences geared toward "speaking" jazz—they didn't have any jazz "chops."

Providing the basic building blocks of jazz is what this unique approach does for both you and your students. Shelly Berg began this process by authoring a series of instrumental jazz books called "Chop-Monster"—he broke down the "language" of improvisation and jazz into developmentally appropriate pieces. When you put them all together, you get jazz! *Chop-Monster Jr.* is an adaptation of those concepts, made even easier for the elementary general music classroom, grades 3 through 6.

This book breaks down the language of jazz so that you and your students will really experience just what jazz is—the essence of exactly what it is like to get into the style, take wing and soar. *You don't need to have any personal jazz experience to use this book.* All of the examples, all of the modeling is done for you by leading jazz musicians! How cool is that? Your students will hear the "best of the best" play the same things that they will be asked to do—no more worrying about modeling, about how to sequence and scaffold student experience and understanding. It is all here, and it has all been kid-tested and kid-approved! If your music class meets once a week, or every day for 6 weeks, this program can fit your needs—it can be tailored to your class and your students' experience level. The activities are very hands-on, with plenty of opportunity to experiment musically.

Also included in this book are classroom management tips, built-in opportunities for student reflection, meaningful experiences that reinforce new learning each step of the way and links to other curricular areas. If you have always shied away from hands-on jazz activities, now is the time to begin! *Chop-Monster Jr.* is a method for **you** to experience, **along** with your students—a shared learning opportunity scaffolded in such a way that you **all** will feel comfortable.

So, come on a trip of a lifetime! Jump into jazz with *Chop-Monster Jr.* You will not look at jazz in the general music classroom in the same way again. We invite you to let go, and have some fun improvising on the feeling of watching your students grow and learn, by getting messy with the music.
It won't be long before you have a bunch of Chop-Monsters in your classes. Wait until you hear the magic!

Margaret Fitzgerald

Music and Jazz Basics

You may need to review a few basic music terms and concepts with your students before getting started with *Chop-Monster Jr.*:

1. Melody   2. Harmony   3. Rhythm

■ **Melody** is that musical element that we sing or play alone. It is a linear (horizontal) succession of single notes following one after the other, made memorable by contour and repetition.

■ **Harmony** results when two or more pitches (musical notes) are sounded simultaneously, usually creating chords, which are consonant (pleasing) combinations of notes. Harmony is a vertical musical element, although it can be implied by melodic construction. Some chords sound as though they want to move to another chord, while other chords feel anchored in one place. This interaction of chords makes music interesting to listen to.

■ **Rhythm** refers to the placement of notes in time, and their relationship to a beat (pulse). Rhythm is a linear element and is the propulsive engine of melody and harmony. It gives music its energy and personality. Rhythm is often heard in the drums, but you can also create rhythm by clapping your hands, snapping your fingers, or tapping your feet. When rhythms are organized into repeated patterns with strong and weak accents (beats), a meter and a style are born. Jazz music is mostly performed in 4/4 (common time), with four beats per measure.

■ **What makes JAZZ sound like *JAZZ*?**

• The melody is often **embellished, syncopated**, or **varied**, at the performer's discretion. **Bending** or **slurring** from one note to another is also common.

• The harmony may include **more dissonant notes**.

• The **rhythm emphasizes beats 2 & 4,** which gives it a "swinging" feeling.

• Jazz musicians **compose new melodies on the spot** to the same harmony as the song's original melody, and that is called **improvisation**.

There are three things you can practice by yourself that will make teaching the activities in this book much easier. Good news—they are all *very* easy:

(A) You will need to be able to **clap** and **snap** your fingers on accented **beats 2 & 4**:

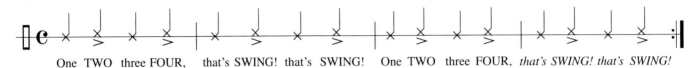

One TWO three FOUR,   that's SWING! that's SWING!   One TWO three FOUR, *that's SWING! that's SWING!*

(B) You will need to understand **swing eighth notes**. I've explained swing eighth notes in a variety of ways over the years, but I find the following is the easiest for young people to grasp: I chant "doodle-dah" to represent a triplet, then transition to "doo-dah" as shown below. If your students go on to play a wind instrument in junior or senior high school, they will already know how to articulate swing eighth notes (thanks to you). A number of the activities in *Chop-Monster Jr.* are built around "doodle-dah" so give yourself a head start and practice it before it's time to teach it. Margaret and Kim expanded on this concept in this text with their kneedle-dah body percussion adaptation, which makes it very clear to elementary students.

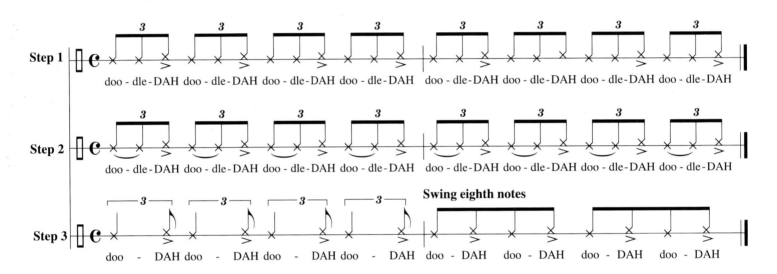

(C) You will need to be able to play a basic "ride-cymbal pattern" with swing eighth notes. The ride cymbal is the largest cymbal in a jazz drummer's kit, and it keeps the musical energy moving forward. Margaret and Kim came up with the chant "gum, bubble gum, bubble gum" to make it easy for children to remember. You'll need to suspend a cymbal on a cymbal stand, so the cymbal can "ride."

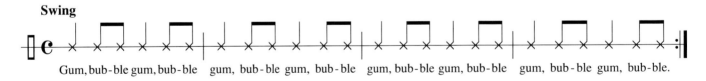

Gum, bub-ble gum, bub-ble   gum, bub-ble gum, bub-ble   gum, bub-ble gum, bub-ble   gum, bub-ble gum, bub-ble.

Well, now that you've got those three concepts down, it's time to get started. Don't be afraid to use the recorded examples to present each new concept, and repeat the backing tracks as often as needed. Aural listening and vocal imitation are fundamental to learning the jazz style—it is how I learned, and it is how all of the jazz masters learned, and it certainly worked for them!

Shelly Berg

Jazz Etiquette

■ Cueing Soloists

Throughout *Chop-Monster Jr.* you will need to cue in soloists. For many of the singing activities you'll see that we suggest using an Orff mallet as a pretend microphone, which is a fun and interactive way for you to cue in students. When students are improvising on barred instruments, you can use traditional conducting cues, count them in, or give non-verbal prompts such as tapping in the palm of your hand during the measure before their entrance. Do what comes naturally to you.

■ Counting Off

Also, the correct way to begin jazz tunes is to give a verbal count-off with a solid snap on beats 2 & 4. Set the tempo and infuse your voice with energy and enthusiasm so students will match that enthusiasm when they begin to play. To do the count-off, say "1 (snap) 2, (snap) 1, 2, 3, 4!" On the *Chop-Monster Jr.* recordings, you will hear Shelly Berg counting off the tracks. Listen and notice how he uses his voice to bring the group in at the correct dynamic level and with the swinging feel that we want students to use. The count-off is really important; you must give the verbal count-off, even in performances.

■ Conducting

On a related topic is the style of conducting jazz groups. Jazz groups are rarely conducted by standing in front of the group and conducting every beat for the whole tune. A baton is not customary, either. There are two schools of thought for jazz ensemble conducting. The first keeps a low profile, counting the song off and staying in front until it seems like the groove is solid and the ensemble is off to a good start. Then the conductor moves to the side and cues in individual parts and soli sections, and cues the soloists, but in general "less is more" when leading jazz groups. The second school of thought views the conductor as the lightning rod of the ensemble and sets the tone and the excitement through his/her musical leadership. The conductor helps to interpret the music through gestures, eye contact and encouragement. With either style, the jazz conductor functions as a coach and gives freedom to musicians to be expressive as they play their improvisations. For the *Chop-Monster Jr.* activities and arrangements, you will function as a jazz conductor, actively encouraging soloists, cueing rhythm section parts, and reminding students of the song forms. You can participate in the arrangements as much as the students! It is a fluid and interactive way to experience the music.

■ Clapping

In jazz we are also free to express ourselves through clapping and giving verbal encouragement or appreciation. This comes from the African-American culture of call-and-response. You and your students should feel free to say things like "Yeah!" "Alright" and "Go!" during and at the end of great solos. Jazz audiences applaud after each soloist improvises, so it is important for you to model applause to your kids and their audience. Applause can even occur during a solo if someone is really showing their chops!

Guided Questions for Reflecting on Listening

Throughout *Chop-Monster Jr.* you will see references to "Guided Questions for Reflecting on Listening." These are questions that encourage higher level thinking and discussion. The questions keep the focus on the students, and encourage them to interact, rather than passively listen to your commentary. We provide the following as a place to start:

- Was the solo musical?
- Did it make musical sense?
- Was it interesting to listen to?
- How did you feel while you were improvising?
- What ideas or feelings were in your head while you were soloing?
- Did your solo have a feeling that you were expressing to the listeners?
- What ideas did you hear in your partner's solos that you might use in your future solos?
- How do you make your solos fit with the singer and the group on the recording?
- What are the musicians on the recording doing that help you to improvise an interesting solo?
- Do you find yourself listening to one instrument more than others?
- What are some of the things you heard that are different?
- Was it cool?
- Was it jazz? Yeah!!

Margaret Fitzgerald   Kimberly McCord

How to Use This Publication

Chop-Monster Jr. is grouped into three units (Rhythm of Jazz, Heart of Jazz, Soul of Jazz), with three parts per unit that teach specific skills for learning how to **play** jazz, such as groove, swing, call-and-response, scat singing, rhythm section, improvising and so on. While there are a variety of excellent jazz appreciation resources available now, which are referenced throughout the text in suggested learning links, this improvisation course focuses on the "doing" and as such, is the first of its kind for classroom music education.

Unit 1: Rhythm of Jazz	Unit 2: Heart of Jazz	Unit 3: Soul of Jazz
Part 1: Grooving in Jazz	Part 1: Communicating in Jazz	Part 1: Cooking in Jazz
Part 2: Responding in Jazz	Part 2: Scatting in Jazz	Part 2: Jamming in Jazz
Part 3: Swinging in Jazz	Part 3: Improvising in Jazz	Part 3: Freedom in Jazz

Each part is organized into activity categories: **Jam Session** (for practice), **Concert Time** (for performance) and **Sitting In** (learning about great jazz masters through suggested learning links to history and literature).

Jam Session

Chop-Monster Jr. lesson activities are presented sequentially, with students vocalizing, moving and transferring what they have learned to un-pitched and pitched instruments. Students learn to scat sing as well as play a variety of rhythm instruments, Orff instruments and Boomwhackers™ tuned percussion tubes, all in a jazz style. Recordings for each lesson activity and the performance pieces are provided on the enclosed CDs.

■ Suggested Percussion Instruments

Substitute as needed.

> 1 ride cymbal (suspended on a stand) with drumstick
> 1 soprano glockenspiel with 2 mallets
> 1 or 2 alto glockenspiel with 2 mallets (last song requires an F♯ bar)
> 1 or 2 alto xylophone with 2 mallets
> 1 bass xylophone with 2 mallets (or a set of bass Boomwhackers)
> 1 set of 8 diatonic Boomwhackers tuned percussion tubes
> 1 set of Octivator™ caps for Boomwhackers (lowers pitch one octave)
> 1 low-pitched drum with soft mallet (e.g., large hand drum, roto-tom, tom-tom)
> 1 pair of rhythm sticks, plus other un-pitched instruments of your choice
> 1 Orff mallet to use as a pretend microphone

■ Call-and-Response Recordings

This teacher's handbook is published with two compact discs (CDs). The call-and-response CD tracks will imbue your students with the language and nuances of jazz improvisation. It is very important that the assimilation of these tracks not be rushed. Our prescription for each track is as follows:

Have students chant and later sing along with the CD until they not only can reproduce each pitch, but also mimic convincingly the rhythm, style and nuance of each melody. This must be accomplished in a "performance" from the beginning to the end of the track, without interruption.

Next, students must be able to transfer and master these same elements through body percussion and on the un-pitched and pitched percussion instruments. This will take longer, as they learn to produce the characteristic sound and articulation.

Finally, you should stay with a track until your better students can freely reproduce the call-and-response melodies in their improvisations. For each summary lesson there is an "open" track for improvisation.

■ Reproducible Worksheet Masters

We've provided 14 reproducible worksheet masters that contain listening maps, photographs of instruments, photographs of jazz masters, and worksheets for guided learning. Permission is granted to duplicate the masters onto transparency film for classroom use, or to make photocopies and distribute to each student.

Concert Time

■ Rhythm Instrument Arrangements and Orff Arrangements

Eight performance pieces are included in *Chop-Monster Jr.* with open sections for call-and-response plus improvisation. Some of the arrangements use rhythm instruments and body percussion; others add Orff classroom instruments or Boomwhackers. All of the arrangements may be performed with or without the CD backing tracks, whatever you prefer. Several of the arrangements have optional piano accompaniment.

Sitting In

Each part of *Chop-Monster Jr.* includes suggested learning links to jazz history and literature through reference sections called **Link to Jazz Masters, Link to Literature** and **Link to History**. Each Link to Jazz Masters provides a brief biography of a great jazz recording artist and suggested listening activities. Each Link to Literature recommends a story book that relates to the jazz masters or the jazz style. Each Link to History provides recommended website links and Episode/Lesson references for respected audio and video resources.

Remember to Have Fun

As you lead your students through these activities, they will find that playing and improvising jazz can be easy and fun, because they will be making use of and developing their inner creativity. And so will you!

Your students learned to speak by imitating family members and friends, and they will learn to improvise the language of jazz in the same manner, imitating the notes and inflections of the call-and-response recordings. Soon these melodies will be their language, spoken in their own unique voices. The more practice and repetition they get the easier and more enjoyable it will be. In the end, they can be the Chop-Monsters!

Have fun.

Grooving in Jazz

- Steady beat in $\frac{4}{4}$
- Jazz swing feel

Preparing for Success

✔ Jam Session

Students will learn to feel a steady beat in $\frac{4}{4}$, and will independently find the jazz groove (swing feel) on beats 2 & 4 through listening, responding, moving and vocalizing to selected musical examples. Students will respond to the jazz groove of 2 & 4 on classroom instruments.

Activity 1: Steady Feet (Marching)
Activity 2: Swinging Feet (That's Swing)
Activity 3: That's Jazz (combine)
Activity 4: *Jazzy Hands* (pass the beat)
Activity 5: *Jazzy Band* (pass the instrument)
Activity 6: *Jazzy Ride* (add ride cymbal)
Link: New Orleans Brass Bands

Vocabulary

Jazz, swing, feel, steady beat, jam, jam session, accent, ride cymbal, drumset

Materials

- *Chop-Monster Jr.* CD1-Tracks 1–7
- Worksheet 1: Musical Instruments
- Worksheet 2: Drums and Jazz
- Ride cymbal with drumstick (a suspended cymbal on a stand and one drumstick)
- F Boomwhacker (an F Boomwhacker tuned percussion tube with Octivator cap)
- Boomwhacker alternatives: clave, beanbag, or plastic shaker

Indicators of Success

Students are successful in finding beats 2 & 4 through movement, vocalizing, playing classroom instruments, listening and responding to selected jazz examples.

♪ Concert Time

Students will demonstrate their internalization of jazz swing feel through independent performance of *Jazzy Ride*.

⊙ Sitting In

Students will learn about the historical development of the jazz swing feel, brass bands and social traditions in New Orleans through suggested learning links.

Unless specified, you will need to supply the referenced audio or video recordings.

Link to Jazz Masters

"Oh, Lady Be Good," George Gershwin, Ira Gershwin. *Eureka Brass Band: New Orleans Funeral and Parade*, Eureka Brass Band. American Music Records, audio recording. www.jazzology.com

"Oh, Lady Be Good," recorded by Jones-Smith Incorporated is featured on *Ken Burns Jazz: The Story of America's Music*, Disc 2, Columbia/Legacy 5-CD set (from *Essential Count Basie Vol. 1*, Columbia/Legacy), audio recording. www.legacyrecordings.com

"Oh, Lady Be Good," George Gershwin, Ira Gershwin. *Best of Early Basie*, Count Basie Orchestra. Decca, audio recording. www.vervemusicgroup.com

Link to Literature

The Jazz of Our Street, Fatima Shaik, pictures by E. B. Lewis. New York: Dial Books for Young Readers/Penguin Putnam Inc., 1998. www.penguinputnam.com

Link to History

Archival film featuring "Oh, Lady Be Good," recorded by Artie Shaw and His Orchestra, 1939, is included in *Jazz: A Film by Ken Burns*, Episode 6, Florentine Films/PBS/Warner Home Video, 10-episode video series (also DVD). www.pbs.org/jazz

Jazz for Young People Curriculum, Lesson 1, Marsalis, New York: Jazz at Lincoln Center, 2002, teaching curriculum with 30 student guides, 10-CD set audio recordings and video recording. www.jazzatlincolncenter.org

✔ Jam Session

Introduction

*"We are going to explore an exciting style of music called **jazz**. Who can tell me what they already know about jazz?"*

Students should give a variety of answers such as "You can dance to it," "It is fun," or "It is happy music."

Reproducible Worksheet 1: Musical Instruments

Optional: Make transparency from Worksheet 1 and show/discuss instruments commonly played by jazz musicians.

*"Jazz is fun to move and dance to because of a special rhythmic feel called **swing**. Let's listen to a jazz tune that features that great quality called swing. As you listen to the music, tap two fingers in your opposite palm on beats 1, 2, 3, 4."*

CD-1 Track 1

Swinging

Play CD1-Track 1 and model tapping a steady beat in the palm of your hand.

*"Tell me a little about what you heard in that jazz recording. What was the beat like? Why do you think jazz musicians say that their music **swings**?"*

Reinforce answers that relate to the swing feel.

Activity 1 / Steady Feet

"Let's see if we can learn to feel the swing of jazz in our feet. To begin, let's make sure we all have steady feet."

CD-1 Track 2

Marching

Using CD1-Track 2 have students march to beats 1, 2, 3, 4, coaching them to feel and maintain a steady beat.

ONE two THREE Four NOT jazz, NOT jazz ONE two THREE Four NOT jazz, NOT jazz

Activity 2 / Swinging Feet

"Now let's see if we can swing our feet."

CD-1 Track 3

That's Swing

Step 1:

Have students listen to CD1-Track 3, *That's Swing*. The feel is now swing, with an emphasis on beats 2 & 4.

One TWO three FOUR, that's SWING! that's SWING! One TWO three FOUR, *that's SWING! that's SWING!*

Step 2:

Listen again to CD1-Track 3 and model tapping all four beats with two fingers in the palm of the opposite hand, inviting students to try it. After listening ask,

"Where does this music make you want to clap? Let's see if you can figure that out while we listen to this again."

Children should be clapping on beats 2 & 4.

Step 3: *Add movement*

- Using CD1-Track 3 again, children move in a circle emphasizing beats 2 & 4 in their improvised movements. Children may count out loud saying, "1, 2, 3, 4," but eventually should be able to internalize the counts and only move.
- Repeat as often as you like and ask children, "Where does the music make you want to move?" Again, focus their attention on the swing feel.
- Once children are comfortable with emphasizing beats 2 & 4 with their movement, repeat and have children change directions every eight measures, or when they hear the melodic instruments change on the recording, to encourage deeper listening.

Step 4: *Optional*

Ask children to choose partners. Using CD1-Track 3 again, children mirror their partner's movement to beats 2 & 4, for eight measures.

- Partner 1 starts as the leader and improvises a movement for eight measures on beats 2 & 4. Examples: Twists at waist, snap fingers, bend at knees.
- Partner 2 joins in and mirrors Partner 1's movements.
- Partners switch leaders every 8 measures, or when they hear the melodic instruments change on the recording.

Tip from Margaret

Children with disabilities who have trouble with gross motor movement activities are probably the same children who also have problems with dance. In my classroom, I tend to "drift" through the class and tap such students on the shoulder on beats 2 & 4 along with the verbalization of "rest STEP rest STEP" or "rest SWING rest SWING" or similar. You should use whatever words you are comfortable using. Sometimes the physical tapping along with aural/oral input can help. For children with physical challenges, offer a rhythm instrument to play on beats 2 & 4.

Tip from Kim

CD1-Track 3, *That's Swing*, is a fun way to bring children into the music room, or to get them seated on chairs or on the floor. Lead a line of students through the room, moving, clapping or snapping to beats 2 & 4. Encourage good listening skills by cueing students to sit down with the "Basie ending," a common tag ending heard on many recordings by the Count Basie Orchestra.

Activity 3 / *That's Jazz*

"Now we're going to compare our marching feet to our swinging feet."

CD-1
 Track 4 ***That's Jazz***

Step 1:

With or without CD1-Track 4, combine *Marching* and *That's Swing* to model the *That's Jazz* chant.

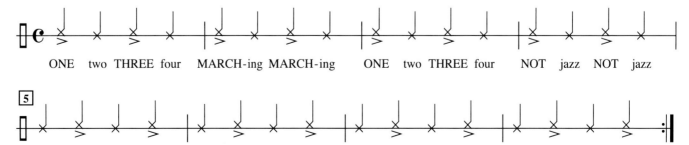

Step 2:

- Children chant along with teacher for first part of chant: "ONE two THREE four MARCH-ing MARCH-ing ONE two THREE four NOT jazz NOT jazz."
- Children then echo by themselves to the second part of chant: "one TWO three FOUR that's SWING that's SWING one TWO three FOUR that's JAZZ that's JAZZ."
- Children say the entire chant.

Step 3: Add movement

- Using CD1-Track 4, demonstrate marching to the first four bars of *That's Jazz,* emphasizing beats 1 & 3, then switch emphasis during the last four bars to beats 2 & 4.
- Students march in place, switching emphasis from march feel 1 & 3 to swing feel 2 & 4.
- Add chant when movement feels more secure.

Step 4:

- Children are in a circle and march one direction for the first four bars emphasizing beats 1 & 3 and then switch directions for the second four bars emphasizing beats 2 & 4.
- Gradually add the chant words.

Repeat over several lessons.

Step 5: Peer-Assessment

CD-1
Track 5

That's Jazz,
Backing Track

- Once children are secure with the *That's Jazz* chant, group them in several small groups or pairs for a peer-assessment activity.
- Use the "backing" Track 5 (no lyrics recorded) and have the groups take turns for eight measures each demonstrating how well they can differentiate the march feel (emphasizing beats 1 & 3 for four measures) and the swing feel (emphasizing beats 2 & 4 for four measures).
- Groups may demonstrate using body percussion or un-pitched rhythm instruments to play march beats 1 & 3, and swing beats 2 & 4. Choose instruments such as rhythm sticks that don't sustain a tone for long.
- Once students are comfortable with the group activity, form a circle and have them take turns individually.

Tip from Margaret

Just like anything else new, this "feel" for 2 & 4 might take some kids longer than others to internalize. I find that kids who listen to rap and rock music can already "feel" the 2 & 4 and need to put that feel into a new frame of reference—music class and jazz!

Activity 4 / *Jazzy Hands*

*"Let's play a game called **Jazzy Hands**. In this game the object is to pass the swing beats 2 & 4 to the person next to you."*

Step 1:

Sit with children in a circle. Hands are out to the side with palms up, elbows bent close to the waist.

"Place your right hand, palm up, on top of your neighbor's left hand. Place your left hand, palm up, underneath your neighbor's right hand. Everyone's right hand should now be on top of somebody's left hand."

The result is a continuous chain of hands.

Step 2:

Count aloud "one TWO three FOUR one" and begin the game by clapping your *right* hand to your neighbor student's *right* hand on beat 2. Each student will pass the beat with their right hand across the front of their body. Say "one TWO three FOUR rest PASS rest PASS" or "one TWO three FOUR that's SWING that's SWING" or other verbal prompts to help students focus on passing on beats 2 & 4.

CD-1
Track 6

Jazzy Hands

Step 3:

Practice *Jazzy Hands* activity with CD1-Track 6 until students are comfortably passing beats 2 & 4.

Step 4:

Play CD1-Track 6 once again, and have students creatively walk around the room finding beats 2 & 4, perhaps suggesting they act like cool middle/junior-high schoolers, snapping to beats 2 & 4. Observe how well they have internalized the concept of jazz swing.

Activity 5 / *Jazzy Band*

*"We're swinging so well, we're going to **jam** in a game called **Jazzy Band**. A **jam session** is when musicians get together to play for fun. The object of this activity is to pass an instrument around our circle, feeling swing beats 2 & 4."*

This activity involves passing an F Boomwhacker tuned percussion tube with Octivator cap (the cap lowers the pitch an octave) and *slapping it horizontally* on the floor on beats 2 & 4. If your music classroom is not carpeted, then instruct students to hold the Boomwhacker vertically at a 90 degree angle and tap the bottom of the Octivator cap on the floor.

If you don't have access to Boomwhackers (readily available through classroom music suppliers), use a clave, bean bag, or plastic shaker...any durable instrument that is easy to grasp and makes an interesting sound when it is hit horizontally on the floor.

CD-1

Jazzy Band

Step 1:

Ask students to *kneel* in a circle. Using CD1-Track 7, pass the instrument around the circle:

- Student 1: Grab/pick up instrument on beat 1, pass right and strike instrument on floor on beat 2,
- Student 2: Grab/pick up instrument on beat 3, pass right and strike instrument on floor on beat 4.
- Repeat around the circle.

If necessary, use this verbal prompt: "pick PLAY pick PLAY," or "rest TWO rest FOUR." If students lose beats 2 & 4 during this activity, stop students while the recording continues to play and ask them to listen. Then bring them in by counting off, "one TWO ready PLAY" (emphasizing the "TWO" and the "PLAY").

Step 2:

Repeat activity and continue to pass the instrument around the circle but have students whisper, then internalize, "rest PASS rest PASS" or "rest PLAY rest PLAY," or "that's SWING that's SWING."

Step 3: *Optional*

Using CD1-Track 7 again, pass an imaginary beat around the circle, rather than the musical instrument.

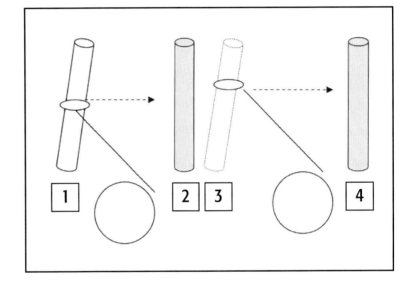

Tip From Kim

When students can start and stop on cue in the *Jazzy Band,* they are ready to move on. This might feel like a lot of repetition on beats 2 & 4, but the activities are varied and should hold your students' interest. Don't rush through this part. It is essential for students to be comfortable with the material before going on to the next step. You need to decide how to sequence these activities and use them in a way that makes sense to you; you are the expert with your own students.

♪ Concert Time

Activity 6 / *Jazzy Ride*

*"The drumset is an important part of any jazz group, especially the **ride cymbal**, which is a cymbal suspended on top of a stand. Listen closely to the way the drummer plays the ride cymbal."*

CD-1
Track 7

Jazzy Band
Play CD1-Track 7 again and have students listen.

"How would you describe the sound the ride cymbal makes? Let's add a ride cymbal to
***Jazzy Band**—and call it **Jazzy Ride**."*

Step 1:

On your ride cymbal, demonstrate the following basic swinging eighth-note ride-cymbal pattern used throughout *Chop-Monster Jr.*, along with the chant "gum, bubble gum, bubble bum, bubble gum…" Jazz drummers play many variations on this basic swing rhythm, so it is a great place to start.

Note: We will explore the triplet subdivision of "swing eighth notes" in subsequent *Chop-Monster Jr.* activities. For now, the chant will help students internalize the sound of the ride cymbal part by rote. In *Chop-Monster Jr.*, we teach many concepts by rote so the jazz language becomes internalized, using chants to help kids remember what the parts sound like.

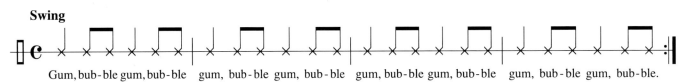

Step 2:

Play CD1-Track 7 and have children pass an F Boomwhacker (as you did in the *Jazzy Band* activity), while you play the ride cymbal part.
Ask for volunteer cymbal players and have students take turns.

Tip from Kim

The swing ride cymbal part will appear in other *Chop-Monster Jr.* activities so it is a good idea for you to become comfortable playing it. Its swinging groove creates a flavor and sound unique to jazz. All children should be encouraged to play the cymbal part, too.

Tip from Margaret

You will usually find at least one student who can reliably play the swing ride cymbal part. One of the problems at first with this tricky little rhythm is that the kids shift beats or change the accent. Be patient in guiding them back on track. It is a great deal easier if you walk up to them and just say "gum, bubble gum, bubble gum" until they are secure. The key is getting the first "gum" on the correct beat.

⊙ Sitting In

The following activities reference resources that are not included with *Chop-Monster Jr.*, such as audio and video recordings and children's literature. We offer these lesson-enrichment ideas to help increase student awareness about the lives and contributions of the great jazz masters.

Link to Jazz Masters: The Drumset and Jazz

New Orleans Brass Bands

"New Orleans brass bands became popular in the early 1900s and are one of the strong roots of jazz. The bands were hired for occasions such as funerals, parades and parties. The bands marched through neighborhood streets playing marches and other popular songs, improvising their parts as they went along. Those who were listening often followed the bands, dancing to the music. The dancers were referred to as the Second Line *since the musicians were the first line. Brass bands remain popular in New Orleans today.*

"The drumset was developed and used for the first time in early jazz groups. Previous to drumsets, brass marching bands in New Orleans generally used two or three musicians to play snare drum, bass drum, and cymbals. Sometimes the bass drum would have a cymbal attached at the top and that player would play both the bass drum and the cymbal, which resulted in the bands having a different sound than traditional marching bands. As time went on, the cymbal became a very important part of the jazz sound."

Teacher's Guide to Listening Activity

Drumset and Jazz

Reproducible Worksheet 2: Drumset and Jazz

Listening: Two versions of Oh, Lady Be Good

- Locate a recording of "Oh, Lady Be Good" by the Eureka Brass Band (*Eureka Brass Band: New Orleans Funeral and Parade*, American Music Records).
- Locate a recording of "Oh, Lady Be Good" by Jones-Smith Incorporated on Disc 2, *Ken Burns Jazz: The Story of America's Music*, Columbia/Legacy (or *Best of Early Basie*, Decca/Verve Music Group).
- This activity will compare the Eureka Brass Band and Jones-Smith Incorporated recordings.

Step 1:

Distribute photocopies of Worksheet 2 to students. Play the Eureka Brass Band recording for approximately 30 seconds (fade out recording at the end of a phrase) and ask students to reflect on the drum sounds.

Step 2:

"Now listen to the whole song. It is called 'Oh, Lady Be Good.' Listen for the drum sounds which include cymbals."

Play Eureka Brass Band recording.

Step 3:

"How do the Eureka Brass Band's drums sound like drums in a marching band? How do the Eureka Brass Band's drums sound like drums in a jazz group? We are going to listen to a recording of the same song performed by a jazz group. How do you think the drums will sound different on this recording?"

Change CDs and listen to the second version of "Oh, Lady Be Good" by Jones Smith Incorporated (featuring Count Basie on piano).

Step 4:

"Now that you have heard the jazz band version, how do the drums sound to you? Do they sound like drums in a marching band? Do you notice the cymbal? How does the cymbal sound different in the marching band and jazz band?"

Step 5:

On the worksheet, have children write in their own words what they think about the drums in the marching band and the drums in the jazz band.

New Orleans Brass Bands

Link to Literature
The Jazz of Our Street
Read aloud *The Jazz of Our Street* by Fatima Shaik with pictures by E.B. Lewis (Dial Books for Young Readers/Penguin Putnam Inc.). The book is a wonderful introduction to New Orleans style brass bands.

Optional: Read along to recordings featured on the compact disc *Eureka Brass Band: New Orleans Funeral and Parade* (American Music Records AMCD-70), beginning with "Lady Be Good" and continuing through "Tell Me Your Dream and Sing On."

Link to History
Jazz: A Film by Ken Burns
Watch Episode 1 of *Jazz: A Film by Ken Burns* to learn about the New Orleans roots of jazz. Watch Episode 6 to see and hear the Artie Shaw Orchestra with Artie Shaw on clarinet, playing "Oh, Lady Be Good."

Jazz at Lincoln Center: *Jazz for Young People Curriculum*
New Orleans Lesson 1 of this curriculum highlights brass marching bands and the use of call-and-response in music played in the early part of the 20th century. Wynton Marsalis talks about the brass bands and the evolution to small jazz combos in New Orleans. *Jazz for Young People Curriculum*, Marsalis, New York: Jazz at Lincoln Center, 2002, compact discs/teacher's guide/student guides.

Websites:

Jazz: A Film by Ken Burns
Biographies, discographies, and other jazz history facts.
www.pbs.org/jazz

Jazz @ Lincoln Center
Information on the Lincoln Center Jazz Orchestra, and the *Jazz for Young People Curriculum*.
www.jazzatlincolncenter.org

Louisiana State Museum
Information on the Eureka Brass Band and a sound clip to listen to.
http://lsm.crt.state.la.us/audio/brass.htm

New Orleans Jazz Club Vintage Broadcasts
Sound clips of instruments in the New Orleans brass bands.
http://lsm.crt.state.la.us/audio/glossary.htm

Dixieland Jazz
This New Orleans Traditional Jazz site has lots of information and photographs of the early New Orleans Brass Bands.
http://www.nfo.net/.WWW/JO.html

Jazz Roots
Photos and information on early jazz.
www.jass.com

Tip from Margaret

If you're not a "jazz person" like me, it takes a while to feel comfortable enough to model the jazz style. Don't be afraid to use the CD tracks to get your own comfort level higher! Practice in your car driving with the windows rolled up, singing by yourself. Once you are comfortable, speak in "swing" to students. To do so, modulate your voice on beats two and four like this:

Let's GO, let's GO, move your FEET with the BEAT

I first practiced the above with the tempo at MM ♩ = 90. When I tried to go faster, it didn't work— it just didn't come naturally to me. But I kept practicing, and now it isn't hard for me anymore!

Responding in Jazz

- Internalize jazz swing feel
- Call-and-response

Preparing for Success

✔ Jam Session

Students will demonstrate swing feel and their understanding of call-and-response through listening, responding, movement and vocalizing to selected recorded musical examples. Students will learn the names of famous jazz masters.

Activity 1: Chop-Monster Groove
Activity 2: Jazz Name Game
Activity 3: *Louis Armstrong* (call-and-response)
Activity 4: *That's Jazz,* Call-and-Response
Activity 5: *Jazz-Ma-Tazz* (ABA portion)
Link: Louis Armstrong

Vocabulary

Chops, monster, groove, call-and-response, scat, Louis Armstrong

Materials

- *Chop-Monster Jr.* CD1-Tracks 6–10
- Worksheet 3: Jazz Performers
- Worksheet 4: Map of Africa
- Worksheet 5: "Rockin' Chair" Listening Map
- Ride cymbal with drumstick
- Alto xylophone with 2 mallets (E, F, B♭)
- Bass xylophone with 2 mallets (C octaves)
  or C Bass Boomwhacker, or both

Indicators of Success

Students will perform the Chop-Monster Groove and feel swing beats 2 & 4. Students will begin to internalize the ride cymbal swing pattern and understand the concept of call-and-response.

♪ Concert Time

Students will demonstrate their understanding of swing feel and call-and-response through independent performance of the ABA portion of *Jazz-Ma-Tazz*.

☉ Sitting In

Students will learn about Louis Armstrong and the use of call-and-response in jazz through suggested learning links.

Unless specified, you will need to supply the referenced audio or video recordings.

Link to Jazz Masters

"Rockin' Chair," Hoagy Carmichael. Louis Armstrong with Jack Teagarden, *Ken Burns Jazz: The Story of America's Music,* Disc 3, Columbia/Legacy, 5-CD set (from *The Complete RCA Victor Recordings*, BMG), audio recording.
www.legacyrecordings.com

Link to Literature

If I Only Had a Horn: Young Louis Armstrong, Roxanne Orgill, illustrated by Leonard Jenkins. Boston: Houghton Mifflin Company, 1997.
www.houghtonmifflinbooks.com

Link to History

Archival film featuring "Rockin' Chair" performed by Louis Armstrong and Jack Teagarden on the television special *Timex All Star Jazz Show,* 1957 is included in *Jazz: A Film by Ken Burns,* Episode 8, Florentine Films/PBS/Warner Home Video, 2000, 10-episode video series (also DVD).
www.pbs.org/jazz

Jazz for Young People Curriculum, Lesson 3, Marsalis, New York: Jazz at Lincoln Center, 2002, teaching curriculum with 30 student guides, 10-CD set audio recordings and video recording.
www.jazzatlincolncenter.org

✓ Jam Session

Introduction

*"Great jazz musicians have great **chops**. Your chops are your skills: how good you are at playing instruments, singing and creating music of your own. When a musician is really good at these things, they have great chops, and the other musicians call him or her a **monster**. We're going to learn the Chop-Monster Groove."*

Activity 1 / Chop-Monster Groove

CD-1
Track 6

Chop-Monster Groove
(same track as *Jazzy Hands*)

- Teach students how to do the Chop-Monster Groove as diagrammed below.
- Play CD1-Track 6 and have students do the Chop-Monster Groove while listening carefully.
- Claps should match the hi-hat cymbals closing on beats 2 & 4. If desired, explain that a hi-hat is two cymbals that close together when a drummer presses and releases a foot pedal. Unit 3/Part 1 discusses the role of the jazz rhythm section in detail. For now, students just need to learn how to listen for, and feel, beats 2 & 4.

Beat 1: Tap two fingers lightly in palm of opposite hand

Beat 2: Clap

Beat 3: Tap two fingers lightly in palm of opposite hand

Beat 4: Clap

Repeat, accenting beats 2 & 4.

Activity 2 / Jazz Name Game

Step 1:

Seat students in a circle and find one student with a two-syllable name such as Spencer. Chant the name, emphasizing the first part of the name (SPEN-cer).

Step 2:

"What would it be like if I said 'spen-CER' instead?"

Modulate your voice higher on the second syllable for emphasis.
"It's similar to when a parent calls you, and you know you are in trouble—you will hear your name called like this: spen-CER!"

Ask students to chant, emphasizing the second part of the name (spen-CER).

Step 3:

"Which way sounds the most jazzy?"

Students should easily identify: spen-CER.

Jazz Name Game
(same track as *Jazzy Band*)

Step 4:

Play CD1-Track 7, model Chop-Monster Groove, and chant the name of one of your students along with the recording, emphasizing the second syllable of the name. Repeat, using different children's names.

Activity 3 / *Louis Armstrong*

"Let's learn the name of a great jazz performer, **Louis Armstrong**. Louis grew up in New Orleans in the early 1900s and played the cornet at a time when jazz was becoming popular. His way of playing jazz was bold and expressive."

Louis Armstrong

Step 1:

Using CD1-Track 8, tap/clap the Chop-Monster Groove, and have children imitate the vocalist on the recording singing 1-bar phrases from the song *Louis Armstrong* shown below.

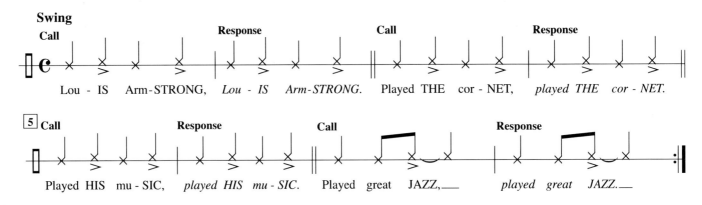

Note: Syncopation, as in measures 7 and 8, is characteristic in jazz. Your students will easily imitate syncopated rhythms through call-and-response.

Step 2: Define Call-and-Response

"Having a leader 'call' and others imitate and 'respond' is referred to as **call-and-response**, the musical name for question and answer. That is what we were doing with our Louis Armstrong song. It is an important element of jazz music."

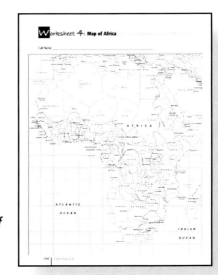

Reproducible Worksheet 4: Map of Africa
Use a classroom world map or create a transparency from Worksheet 4 and show Ghana and the area around Ghana on a world map.

"Call-and-response goes back in history to West Africa where it is a common musical device. Many Africans that were forced into slavery in America were from West Africa. After emancipation, a large number of their descendants settled in New Orleans. Some of these descendants became jazz musicians. As a result, we hear call-and-response in jazz music. Today, call-and-response is heard in many styles of music, not just jazz."

Activity 4 / *That's Jazz*, Call-and-Response

*"Let's use call-and-response with our **That's Jazz** marching and swinging chant."*

CD-1
Track 5

That's Jazz,
Backing Track

Step 1:

> Use CD1-Track 5 *That's Jazz*, Backing Track from Unit 1/Part 1/Activity 1.

Step 2:

> During this call-and-response adaptation of *That's Jazz*, it is important to have children tap/clap the Chop-Monster Groove with the music so they can tell both aurally and kinesthetically when to accent beats 1 & 3 during the march feel and when to accent beats 2 & 4 during the swing feel.

"This time, I will be the Leader and you will respond to my 'call' like this:"

> During march section, teacher calls:
> ONE, two, THREE, four, MARCH-ing, MARCH-ing,
> ONE, two, THREE, four
> Students take turns around the circle responding:
> > NOT jazz, NOT jazz.

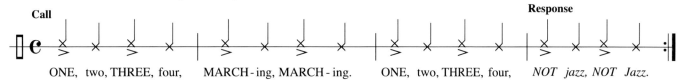

> During swing section, teacher calls:
> one, TWO, three, FOUR, that's SWING, that's SWING
> one, TWO, three, FOUR
> and students take turns around the circle responding:
> > that's JAZZ, that's JAZZ!

♪ Concert Time

Activity 5 / *Jazz-Ma-Tazz*

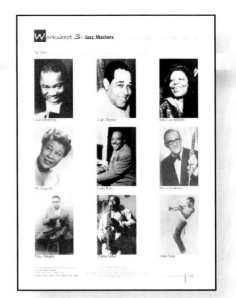

Reproducible Worksheet 3: Jazz Performers

Distribute photocopies of Worksheet 3 and review the listed jazz performers and the instruments that they played.

*"Now we're going to learn and perform a song called **Jazz-Ma-Tazz**. The first section, which we'll call the 'A' section, will have parts to play and sing. The second section, which we'll call the 'B' section, uses call-and-response to learn the names of some famous jazz performers."*

CD-1
Track 9

Jazz-Ma-Tazz,
Performance Model, for complete ABACADA form

CD-1
Track 10

Jazz-Ma-Tazz,
Backing Track, for sections ABA (and ADA, optional)
If you do not have Orff instruments, this activity may be performed with body percussion only, or with voices only. The entire song form is ABACADA. However, this activity teaches only sections A and B in ABA form. (Section C and the entire ABACADA song form are taught in Unit 1/Part 3.) If desired, play CD1-Track 9 to model the entire song.

Step 1: Teach "A" section vocal part

- Tap/clap Chop-Monster Groove.
- Teach "A" section melody by rote.

Step 2: Teach "A" section ride cymbal part

- Rub hands together to create the ride cymbal swing pattern.
- Transfer to cymbal. Have students take turns on the ride cymbal.

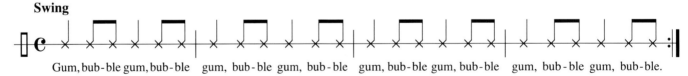

- Combine ride cymbal part with melody and Chop-Monster Groove.

Step 3: Teach "A" section Orff parts

See *Jazz-Ma-Tazz* Orff arrangement following Step 6. Teach alto xylophone and bass xylophone Orff parts by using body percussion:

- Bass Xylophone (or "C" bass Boomwhacker) part patschen.
- Alto Xylophone part clap.
- Transfer to instruments.

Have students perform melody with ride cymbal, Chop-Monster Groove and Orff parts.

Tip From Margaret

I have found that Boomwhackers sound a lot better and louder if you play them on carpeting or carpet squares. I ALWAYS use the Octivator caps because it makes them less "thwacky" sounding. If using a Boomwhacker for this activity, hold it upright with the octivator cap on the bottom. The octivator cap is the part that hits the rug.

Step 4: "B" section call-and-response chant

Teach first verse of the B section by rote, calling composer names and having children respond by imitating your exact vocal inflection. (Modulate your voice higher on the capitalized portion of words).

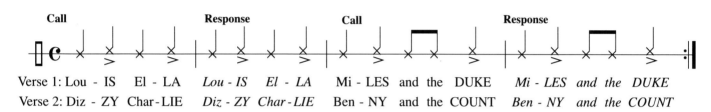

Verse 1: Lou - IS   El - LA   *Lou - IS   El - LA*   Mi - LES and the DUKE   *Mi - LES and the DUKE*
Verse 2: Diz - ZY Char-LIE   *Diz - ZY Char-LIE*   Ben - NY and the COUNT *Ben - NY and the COUNT*

Names referenced in Section B are for the following jazz artists:

Louis Armstrong
Ella Fitzgerald
Miles Davis
Duke Ellington

Step 5:

Using CD1-Track 10, perform sections in ABA form.

Step 6:

Once children are secure with the ABA form, use CD1-Track 10 and perform sections ADA. (Section C will be taught in Unit 1/Part 3). Section D is a call-and-response section similar to section B, using the second verse which features different jazz master names.

Names referenced in Section D are for the following jazz artists:

Dizzy Gillespie
Charlie Parker
Benny Goodman
Count Basie

Jazz-Ma-Tazz

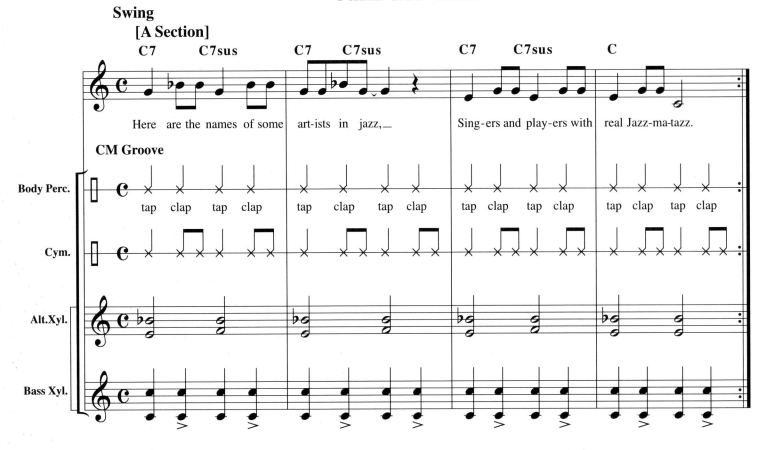

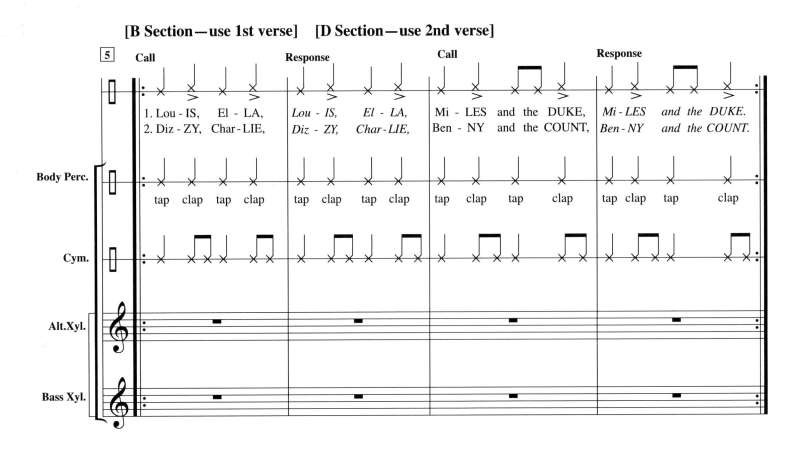

Jazz-Ma-Tazz ABA (optional ADA with second verse)

"C" section notation appears in Unit 1/Part 3

💿 Sitting In

The following activities reference resources that are not included with *Chop-Monster Jr.*, such as audio and video recordings and children's literature. We offer these lesson-enrichment ideas to help increase student awareness about the lives and contributions of the great jazz masters.

Link to Jazz Masters: Call-and-Response with Louis Armstrong

Louis Armstrong (1901–1971)

"Louis Armstrong was born in 1901. He was the first famous person in jazz. He played the trumpet and sang. He grew up in New Orleans hearing older people using call-and-response as they sang and played music, so that is how he learned. Louis was nicknamed Dippermouth and Satchmo (derived from satchel mouth) because he had a big, happy smile. We're going to listen to a recording of Louis Armstrong and a trombonist and singer named Jack Teagarden using call-and-response in a musical conversation."

- Discuss with students how it is possible to "sing" a conversation. Then, "Let's try that!" Tell them you will sing a question to one student, and that student will sing back their response.
- Sing to one student "What month is your birthday?
- The student sings back their reply.
- Sing to the same student again, "Sing the date back to me."
- The student sings back their reply.
- Do a few questions like this between you and several other students.

Louis Armstrong

Teacher's Guide to Listening Activity

Call-and-Response with Louis Armstrong

Reproducible Worksheet 5: Rockin' Chair Listening Map

Listening: Rockin' Chair
The listening map for "Rockin' Chair" matches the recording by Louis Armstrong with Jack Teagarden included on Disc 3, *Ken Burns Jazz: The Story of America's Music* (Columbia/Legacy). The song is also featured on *The California Concerts*, Louis Armstrong (GRP) and in Episode 8 of *Jazz: A Ken Burns Film* (PBS Home Video).

"In this recording called 'Rockin' Chair,' you will hear Louis Armstrong and Jack Teagarden having a call-and-response conversation about being old in their rocking chairs. The call-and-response happens when one person tells his story and the other person makes comments as he is listening."

Step 1:

Distribute photocopies of "Rockin' Chair" Listening Map.

Vocabulary used in "Rockin' Chair"

Chariot's a comin'– he feels like it's almost time to die and ride the chariot to heaven.
Judgment day is here—on the day he dies he believes he'll be judged in heaven about how he behaved in life.
Tan your hide!–get in BIG trouble.

Step 2:

"When you listen to this for the FIRST TIME, write down words that describe what you hear."

- Play "Rockin' Chair" while modeling focused listening: avoid talking over recording or doing anything other than focused listening.
- Pause recording after the first time through the song form.
- Give students a little bit of time to finish writing if they need it.
- Brainstorm with students about more words they can think of to describe how this music sounds, e.g., happy, rough, scratchy, smooth, silky, jumpy.

Tip from Kim

Avoid the temptation to talk over music. It sends a message to kids that it's OK to talk while listening to music. Try to model good listening behavior when asking children to listen to recordings: sit or stand quietly in a focused manner while listening attentively. If you want to say something, "pause' the music before saying it. I like an idea my friend Deb Barber shared with me: when pausing or stopping music, model sensitivity by stopping at the end of a phrase. Deb even turns the volume down at the end of a phrase to fade out. Try modeling focused listening and see how your kids respond.

Step 3:

- Find cue on recording: "Now dig this" before the second vocal section.

"The second vocal section features the same men. Listen and tell me what you think sounds different. Listen carefully to how they use their voices."

- Release pause and play the second verse.
- Pause CD after the second section ends.
- Children should write down describing words for this second section.

Step 4:

"Finally the trumpet and trombone have their own conversation. Write down some describing words for what you hear."

Release pause and play recording to end.

"Bonus question, what is he doing to the flies around the old rockin' chair?"

Step 5:

Play entire recording a second time if students need time to add more describing words to their worksheet.

Step 6:

Discuss using these guiding questions:

"Why did you choose that word? How did they make the sound like that? Who else chose that word? How were the two sets of vocals the same? Different? What was similar between the voices having a conversation and the instruments? What do you suppose the trumpet and trombone were saying? What feeling did you get from this song? If you were to sing this kind of jazzy conversation, would you do anything these men did with their voices? What sounds or ideas would you remember if you sang?"

Step 7:

Point out **scat** singing (scatting) after playing the recording a second time. Scat singing is where a singer uses vocal sounds for musical expression, rather than lyrics. Louis Armstrong scats after "Aunt Harriett in Heaven" and "Judgment Day."

Link to Literature

If I Only Had a Horn: Young Louis Armstrong

Read aloud *If I Only Had a Horn: Young Louis Armstrong* by Roxanne Orgill and illustrated by Leonard Jenkins (Houghton Mifflin Company). The book tells the story of young Louis Armstrong wanting to play the trumpet like his idol King Joe Oliver. The story follows Louis into the Colored Waifs Home where he learned to play the cornet.

Optional: Read along to recordings included on Ken Burns *Jazz: The Story of America's Music,* Disc 1, beginning with "Potato Head Blues" and continuing through "West End Blues."

Link to History

Ken Burns Jazz: The Story of America's Music

Louis Armstrong recorded many great songs that are accessible to children. Listen to Louis scat sing on "Heebie-Jeebies" from *Ken Burns Jazz: The Story of America's Music*, Disc 1 of a 5-CD Boxed Set (Columbia/Legacy). "Heebie-Jeebies" is also included on *Jazz: a Ken Burns Film*, Episode 3 (PBS Home Video).
www.pbs.org/jazz

Jazz at Lincoln Center: *Jazz for Young People Curriculum*

Lesson 3 of the *Jazz for Young People Curriculum* focuses on Louis Armstrong's important contribution to jazz. *Jazz for Young People Curriculum*, Marsalis, New York: Jazz at Lincoln Center, 2002, compact discs/teacher's guide/student guides.
www.jazzatlincolncenter.org

Websites:

Smithsonian Jazz

This site provides photos and useful facts about selected jazz musicians, including Louis Armstrong.
www.smithsonianjazz.org/class/armstrong/la_class_1.asp

Satchmo.net

The official site for the Louis Armstrong House and Archives. Includes a video tour of his house. Investigate the current and past exhibits to learn about Satchmo's world tours and his relationship with his agent, Joe Glaser who managed Louis throughout most of his career.
www.satchmo.net/

Ken Burns Jazz

Numerous biographies of jazz artists, including Louis Armstrong.
www.pbs.org/jazz/biography/artist_id_armstrong_louis.htm

Ken Burns Jazz Kids

"Now and Then" biography section includes a biography of Louis Armstrong.
www.pbs.org/jazz/kids/nowthen/louis.html

Swinging in Jazz

- Triplet undertow to swing feel
- Triplet subdivision aligning with jazz eighth notes
- Swing eighth notes

Preparing for Success

✔ Jam Session

Students will move, chant, sing and use body percussion as they learn about triplet subdivision of swing feel and swing eighth notes. Students will demonstrate their ability to sing and play swing feel. Students will listen to the jazz standard "Take the 'A' Train" and hear contrasting sections of a big band and improvised solos as they follow a listening map.

> Activity 1: *Doodle-Dah Round*
> Activity 2: Kneedle-dah
> Activity 3: *Recess, Yes!*
> Activity 4: Singers-Jazz, Players-Jazz
> Activity 5: *Jazz-Ma-Tazz* (complete form)
> Activity 6: *Jazz Train*
> Link: Duke Ellington

Vocabulary

Doodle-dah, kneedle-dah, triplet, swing feel, improvisation, solos, big band, Duke Ellington

Materials

- *Chop-Monster Jr.* CD1-Tracks 11–21
- Worksheet 3: Jazz Performers
- Worksheet 6: "Take the 'A' Train" Listening Map
- E and G Boomwhackers
- C Bass Boomwhacker

Indicators of Success

Students can perform the *Doodle-Dah Round, Recess, Yes!,* and the complete form of *Jazz-Ma-Tazz.* Students can identify contrasting sections of a big band and improvised solos as they follow a listening map. Students can successfully perform *Jazz Train* with triplet subdivision of swing eighth notes.

♪ Concert Time

Students will demonstrate their understanding of the triplet subdivision in swing feel through independent performance of *Jazz Train.*

💿 Sitting In

Students will learn about the swing era and Duke Ellington and His Orchestra through suggested learning links.

Unless specified, you will need to supply the referenced audio or video recordings.

Link to Jazz Masters

Chop-Monster Jr. CD1-Track 21.

"Take the 'A' Train," Billy Strayhorn. Carmen Bradford, Alfred Publishing, audio recording. www.alfred.com

Link to Literature

Duke Ellington, Andrea Davis Pinkney, illustrated by Brian Pinkney. New York: Hyperion Books for Children, 1998. www.disney.go.com/disneybooks/hyperionbooks

Bring on That Beat by Rachel Isadora. New York: G. P. Putnam's Sons, 2002. www.penguinputnam.com

Link to History

Beyond Category: Duke Ellington Education Kit, Dale Seymour Publications/Smithsonian Institute, 1998. www.pearsonlearning.com

Duke Ellington and Billy Strayhorn collaboration featured in *Jazz: A Film by Ken Burns,* Episode 7, Florentine Films/PBS/Warner Home Video, 10-episode video series (also DVD). www.pbs.org/jazz

Jazz for Young People Curriculum, Lesson 10, Marsalis, New York: Jazz at Lincoln Center, 2002, teaching curriculum with 30 student guides, 10-CD set audio recordings and video recording. www.jazzatlincolncenter.org

Duke Ellington lessons on the MENC web site. www.MENC.org/news/mag/news.html

✓ Jam Session

Introduction

CD-1
Track 11

Doodle-Dah Groove

Bring class into the classroom by moving to CD1-Track 11 and doing
Chop-Monster Groove.

"What is the jazz terminology for what we just did? (Swing.) We are going to learn a way of swinging that Chop-Monsters use. It gives swing its forward motion and it sounds like this:"

Chant "doodle-dah" over and over as you snap your fingers on 2 & 4, or tap/clap
Chop-Monster Groove:

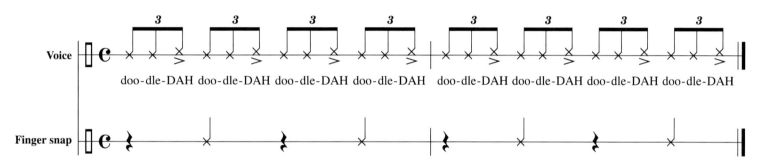

Play CD1-Track 11 again and model "doodle-dah" to the music.
Cue children to join in.

Once you are comfortable with the doodle-dah's, you will want to "ghost" the second syllable slightly ("-dle") because you will eventually model "doo-dah" to create the effect of swing eighth notes, once your students begin to internalize the triplet subdivision. The following rhythmic diagram is for your reference only.

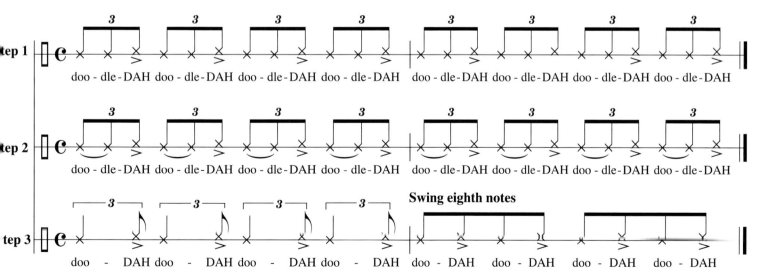

Activity 1 / *Doodle-Dah Round*

Practice chanting doodle-dah before teaching the following activities that culminate in the performance of the *Doodle-Dah Round*. You will teach short sections of the round as independent parts as shown in Steps 1–7 below, using Tracks 12, 13, and 14, then perform the round in its entirety at Step 8. The goal is for students to feel, through rote learning, the rhythmic relationship of one triplet to two swing eighth notes. With this understanding, students will successfully "lock in" to the jazz swing feel.

Doodle-Dah Parts 1, 2 and 3

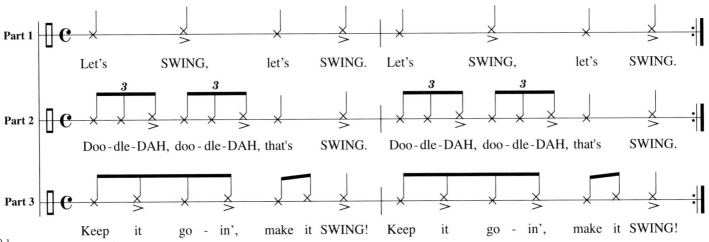

Let's Swing

Step 1: *Let's Swing*

- Play CD1-Track 12.
- Orff barred instrument or Boomwhackers on F should be played quietly on beats 1, 2, 3, 4 to help keep a steady beat.
- Model the Chop-Monster Groove and repeat the "Let's Swing" chant as notated below. Have the class join in.
- Play CD1-Track 12 again and see how well the Group One "Let's Swing" children can swing on their own. Have them chant the "Let's Swing" part with the Chop-Monster Groove.

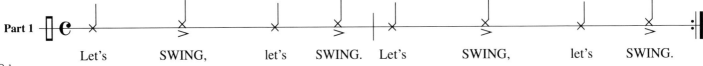

Doodle-Dah, Doodle-Dah, That's Swing

Step 2: *Doodle-Dah, Doodle-Dah, That's Swing*

- When children are secure with the "Let's Swing" chant, play CD1-Track 13 and chant the "Doodle-Dah, Doodle-Dah, That's Swing" part.
- Continue steady beat on Orff barred instrument or Boomwhackers on F.
- Continue Chop-Monster Groove.
- Repeat CD1-Track 13 and have students demonstrate their independent understanding.

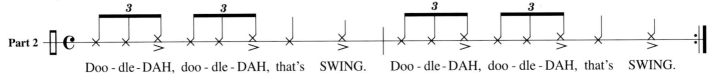

Step 3: Combine

- Split the class into two separate circles: Group One will be the "Let's Swing" circle and Group two will be the "Doodle-dah" circle.
- Continue Chop-Monster Groove and steady beat on F.
- Play CD1-Track 13, and layer in Group Two and then Group One, chanting parts over and over.

Step 4: Switch

- Switch groups so everyone does both parts and hears it together.
- Continue Chop-Monster Groove and steady beat on F.

Step 5: Keep It Going

Keep It Going, Backing Track

- Play backing track, CD1-Track 14.
- Cue the steady beat on F.
- As backing track continues, model the Chop-Monster Groove and the "Keep It Going" chant.
- Have entire class join you with the "Keep It Going" chant.

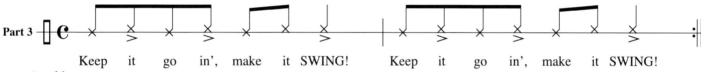

Step 6: Combine

- Once secure, split class into three circles, with Group Three being the "Keep It Going" circle. Have Group Three practice independently with CD1-Track 14.
- Layer in steady beat on F, Chop-Monster Groove, Group Two, and then Group One so all parts are combined.

Step 7: Switch

Repeat Step 6, switching parts so everyone experiences all three parts against each other. Continue the steady beat F. This step may take multiple lessons to master and can't be rushed. Children should visualize, hear and feel all three parts and demonstrate individual independence before moving on to the performance of the round.

Step 8: Doodle-Dah Round

Doodle-Dah Round, **Backing Track**

- The next step is to teach the Doodle-Dah chant as notated below.
- Note the "Let's Swing" and "Keep It Going" phrases are only one measure each.
- When students are comfortably chanting the Doodle Dah chant below, practice performing as a round.
- Use CD1-Track 15 and perform the round, repeating until the end of the track.

Doodle-Dah Round

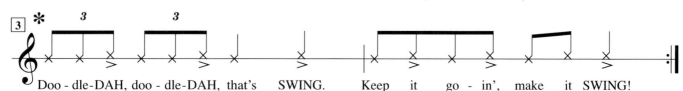

Activity 2 / Kneedle-dah

"Now we're going to use our 'doodle-dah' swinging rhythm in a new way. We'll play it with our hands and call it 'kneedle-dah.'"

Model "kneedle-dah" body percussion while children do Chop-Monster Groove.
You may sit cross-legged, kneel or stand, whichever is more comfortable for you.

Kneedle-dah body percussion:

Lightly slap right thigh with right hand, slap left thigh with left hand, then clap hands together. One "kneedle-dah" coordinates with one triplet. Repeat over and over to create a triplet pattern.

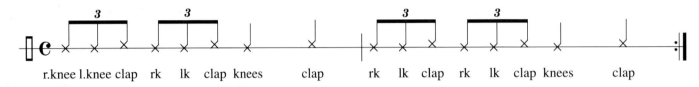

r.knee l.knee clap   rk   lk   clap knees   clap   rk   lk   clap   rk   lk   clap knees   clap

---

Tip from Margaret

Keep the tempo slow and steady to coordinate the kneedle-dah body percussion with the doodle-dah rhythm words. The body percussion helps to clarify where the accents are; children naturally speak louder when they clap. Practice the kneedle-dahs by yourself for a while so you don't accent the wrong notes or words. Make sure you can model speaking the doodle-dah rhythms while you perform the kneedle-dah body percussion before you teach it!

Activity 3 / *Recess, Yes!*

*"Let's learn a new song called **Recess Yes!** It uses the Chop-Monster Groove and our kneedle-dah movement."*

CD-1
Track 16
Recess, Yes!
Performance Model

CD-1
Track 15
Recess, Yes!
Backing Track
(same as *Doodle-Dah Round*)

Recess, Yes!

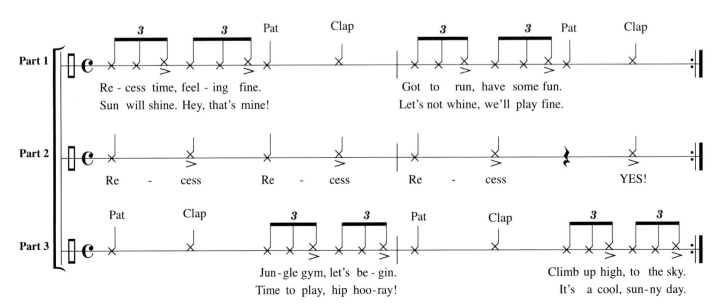

Step 1: Ostinato

Using CD1-Track 16, model *Recess, Yes!*
At a slow tempo, teach the ostinato (Part 2) with the Chop-Monster Groove. Chant
"doodle-dah" quietly if children are rushing the tempo.

Step 2:

Teach part 1 (verse 1) using kneedle-dah body percussion for all triplet figures.

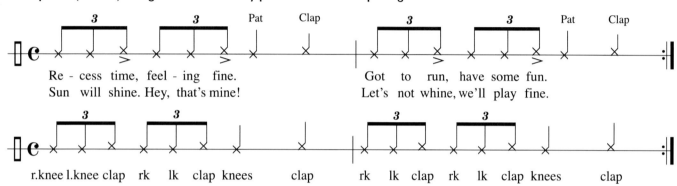

Step 3:

Teach part 3 (verse 1)

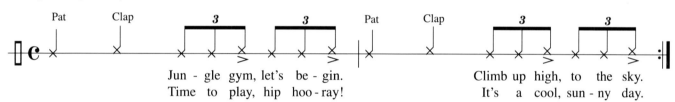

Step 4:

Combine part 1 (verse 1) with part 2 ostinato.

Step 5:

Combine part 3 (verse 1) with part 2 ostinato.

Step 6:

Combine part 1 (verse 2) with part 2 ostinato.

Step 7:

Combine part 3 (verse 2) with part 2 ostinato.

Step 8:

After students can do steps 1 through 7, have them play parts 1 & 3 AT THE SAME
TIME over the part 2 ostinato. The result is a continuous kneedle-dah/triplet pattern
with proper swing eighth-note accents ("do-dah") over a steady ostinato.

CD-1
Track 15

Recess, Yes!

Backing Track (same as *Doodle-Dah Round*)

Step 9:

Perform entire *Recess, Yes!* Chant (page 36) with backing track, CD1-Track 15.

Activity 4 / Singers-Jazz, Players-Jazz

*"We're going to add a section to the song, **Jazz-Ma-Tazz,** but first, let's review what we already know."*

CD-1
Track 10

Backing Track for ABA form (and ADA)

Step 1:

Review *Jazz-Ma-Tazz* sections ABA and ADA from Unit 1/Part 2 with students using
CD1-Track 10, making sure students can securely perform body
percussion/instrument parts. Teach ADA (with the second set of jazz names) if you
did not do so previously.

*"Now let's learn the new section. We'll refer to it as Section C (or 'Singers-Jazz, Players-Jazz'). We're going to learn
Section C using doodle-dah rhythms and kneedle-dah body percussion. Listen to the dynamics carefully."*

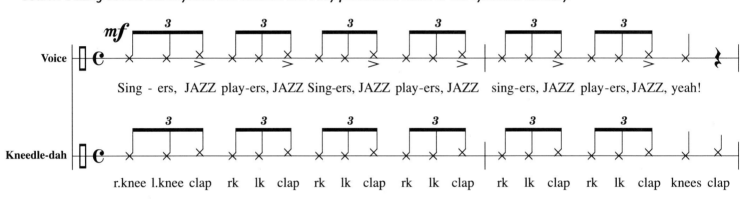

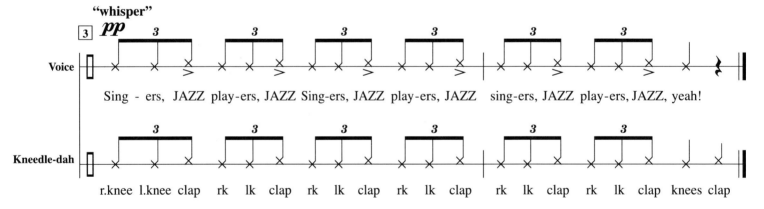

CD-1
Track 17

Backing Track for Section C (Singers-Jazz, Players-Jazz)

Step 2:

- Play CD1-Track 9 to model complete song, if you wish.
- Have students do kneedle-dah body percussion as you model/chant the words,
  "Sing-ers Jazz, Play-ers Jazz" to the movement.

Step 3:

When students are successful with the chanting and body percussion, practice the
Section C chant with CD1-Track 17 and emphasize "Yeah!"
at the end. Do this with kneedle-dah body percussion.

Activity 5 / *Jazz-Ma-Tazz* (Complete)

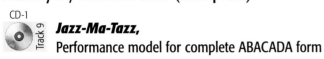

CD-1
Track 9

Jazz-Ma-Tazz,
Performance model for complete ABACADA form

CD-1
Track 18

Jazz-Ma-Tazz,
Backing track for complete ABACADA form
Add in other parts and perform entire ABACADA form
with instruments, with backing track, CD1-Track 18.

Jazz-Ma-Tazz

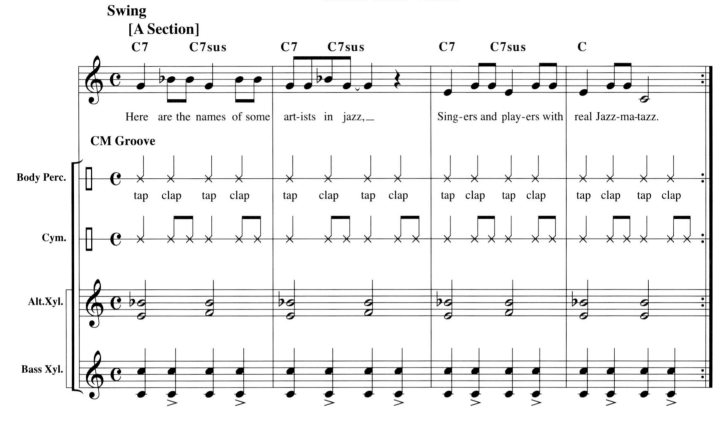

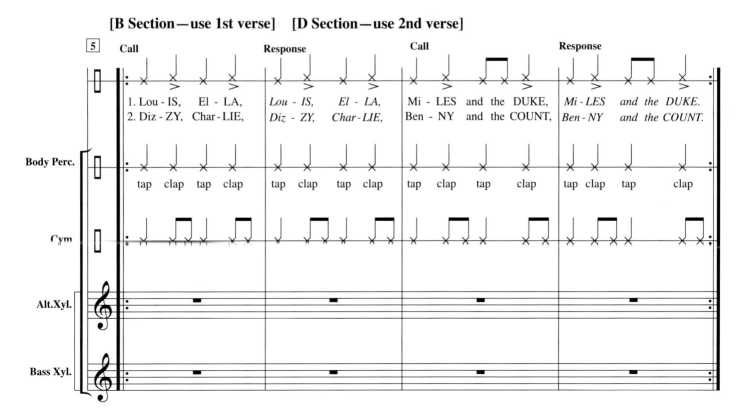

Jazz-Ma-Tazz Section C:

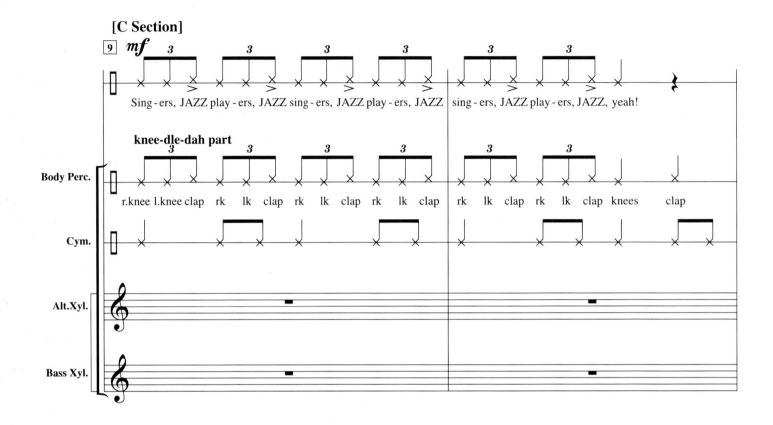

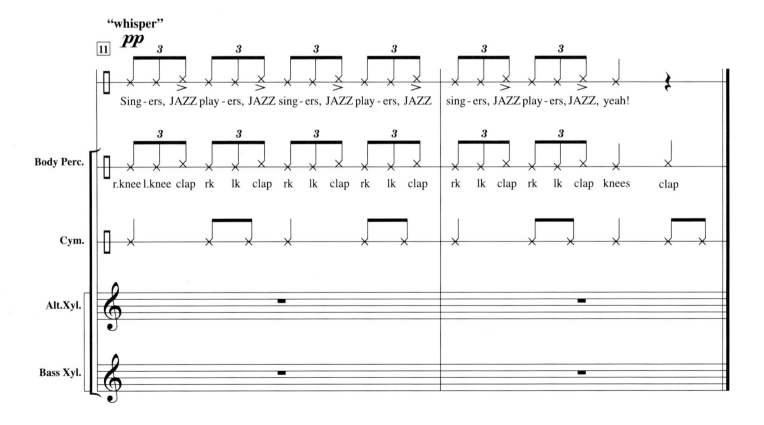

♪ Concert Time

Activity 6 / *Jazz Train*
Notation for complete song is at the end of this section. For teacher reference only; teach by rote.

"The train was a popular way for musicians to travel from city to city in the 1920s and beyond. The rhythm of the train has made its way into many blues and jazz songs. We're going to create a song using our doodle-dah and swing feel called **Jazz Train***."*

CD-1
Track 19

Jazz Train,
Performance Model, with recorded lyrics

CD-1
Track 20

Jazz Train,
Backing Track, no recorded lyrics
The suggested movements are important for getting the parts to fit together. The movements help students learn the rhythms by visualizing, hearing and feeling them. Don't rush through the activity; it may take multiple class meetings to master this. As with all of the activities in *Chop-Monster Jr.,* teach all parts by rote; do NOT write out or photocopy the music notation.

- For your reference, the song form at Letter A is a 12-bar blues. (You don't need to explain that to the students.)
- At Letter B, the students create the sound of a train with 3-part chanting and body percussion parts in a 4-bar vamp.
- We've provided an easy piano accompaniment for you to play for practice and performance. We want you to have some fun learning how to swing, too! If you prefer to use the recorded accompaniments, use CD1-Track 19 for practice and CD1-Track 20 for the final performance. Either way will sound great!

Step 1: Teach melody
- Teach the melody at Letter A by rote (measures 5–16). Teach the "train" parts at Letter B (measures 17–20) as outlined in the following steps, and then combine for performance as described in Step 5.

Step 2: Teach Train Vamp, Part 1
- Teach Part 1 first, using kneedle-dah body percussion with "click-i-ty clack-i-ty."
- Use Chop-Monster Groove throughout.
- Use C bass Boomwhacker to keep a steady beat if you wish.
- Repeat with CD1-Track 19, which is a performance model with recorded lyrics.

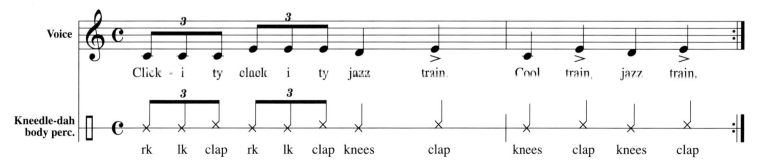

Step 3: Teach Train Vamp, Part 2

- Using CD1-Track 19, teach Part 2 using Chop-Monster Groove while singing "choo-choo."
- The choo-choo swing eighth notes should lock into the clickety-clackity triplet feel.
- Optional: Select two students to play choo-choo swing eighth notes with C and E Boomwhackers (to create an interval of a major 3rd resulting in a C major triad with the vocal part.)

With E and G Boomwackers

Choo-choo, choo-choo.   Choo-choo, choo-choo.   Choo-choo, choo-choo.   Choo-choo, choo-choo.

Step4: Teach Train Vamp, Part 3

- Teach Part 3 using clap on "woo," both hands hit thighs for "ooh," and clap-hold for the long "woo."
- Do this to CD1-Track 19.
- The "woo" emphasizes the flat 7th of this song's C7 chord, and as such is part of the soulful jazz language. Encourage your students to sing it with bluesy inflection.

Woo - ooh woo_____   Woo - ooh woo_____

Step 5: Putting It All Together

- Play Track CD1-19 to model complete song.
- Review melody at Letter A. Continue to have students tap/clap the Chop-Monster Groove while they sing. Continue body percussion for all parts.
- Put all *Jazz Train* parts together and practice with backing track, CD1-20.
- Or, if you are playing the piano accompaniment without the recording, practice adding the introduction and the ending and cueing the students when to sing.
- Put all *Jazz Train* parts together and perform with backing track, CD1-20.
- Optional: using the piano accompaniment performance option, have students create their own independent arrangement, perhaps starting slowly with the clickity clackity Part 1, then getting faster as the imaginary train pulls out of the station. Your students are going to have some very creative ideas! Write out a quick road-map of their arrangement on the board (not music notation, just short reminders like a listening map), and then cue in parts.

Jazz Train

⊙ Sitting In

The following activities reference resources that are not included with *Chop-Monster Jr.*, such as audio and video recordings and children's literature. We offer these lesson-enrichment ideas to help increase student awareness about the lives and contributions of the great jazz masters.

Link to Jazz Masters: Swinging with the Duke

Duke Ellington (1899–1974)

"Duke Ellington was born in Washington D. C. in 1899. His full name was Edward Kennedy Ellington. He played the piano at high school dances and soon started playing at dance halls and parties. He wore flashy clothes and was well liked for his regal and smooth personality. A friend nicknamed him Duke.

*"He moved to New York and formed his own **big band** called the Washingtonians, later called Duke Ellington and His Orchestra. They played at a famous jazz club in Harlem called the Cotton Club for 11 years. A big band is generally comprised of five saxophones, four to five trombones and four to five trumpets, along with a rhythm section of piano, guitar, bass and drums. Many big bands have singers as well. Jazz music played by big bands was very popular for dancing during the Great Depression and beyond. This period in jazz history is often referred to as the swing era, or the golden era. Duke Ellington and His Orchestra toured extensively, performing concerts for jazz fans all around the world.*

Duke Ellington

"Duke Ellington and his composing partner Billy Strayhorn wrote over 2000 pieces of music. Billy Strayhorn wrote the theme song for the Duke Ellington Orchestra called Take the 'A' Train.*"*

Teacher's Guide to Listening Activity

Swinging with the Duke

Reproducible Worksheet 3/Transparency Master: Jazz Performers

Reproducible Worksheet 6: Take the "A" Train Listening Map

CD-1 · Track 21

Listening: *Chop-Monster Jr.* CD1-Track 21, Take the "A" Train

Listen to our recording of "Take the 'A' Train" (CD1-Track 21), or locate a recording of the Duke Ellington Orchestra performing their theme song on Disc 3 of the 5-CD set *Ken Burns Jazz: The Story of America's Music* (Columbia/Legacy).

Step 1:

Play CD1-Track 21 which is our recorded version of "Take the 'A' Train" featuring vocalist Carmen Bradford. Before playing the recording, tell children to pay close attention to the words and see if they can figure out where the train goes.

Step 2:

After listening ask, "Where does the 'A' train go?" Students should identify Harlem.

"Harlem is in New York City. The song says you must take the 'A' train to get to Harlem. The A train is a subway that goes to Harlem. Duke Ellington's band used to play there in the 1930s at a nightclub called the Cotton Club. In addition to hearing Duke's band play great music, people could see dancers and comedians and other entertainment."

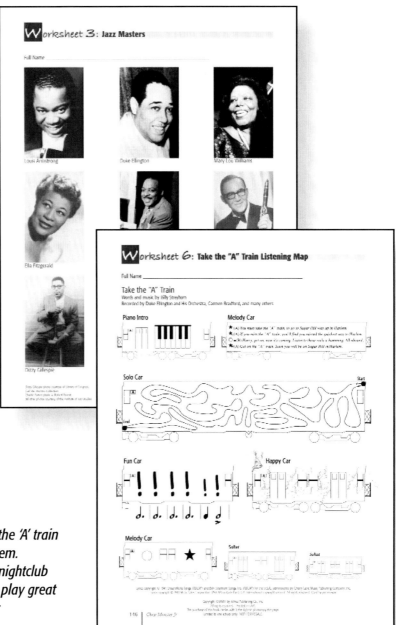

Step 3:

Distribute photocopies of the "Take the 'A' Train" Listening Map and read aloud the song lyrics.
Ask children to read the lyrics with you.

You must take the A train, to go to Sugar Hill way up in Harlem.
If you miss the A train, you'll find you missed the quickest way to Harlem.
Hurry, get on, now it's coming. Listen to those rails a-humming. All aboard,
Get on the A train. Soon you will be on Sugar Hill in Harlem.

Step 4:

- Before playing CD1-Track 21 again, instruct children that they will follow the listening map with a finger while listening to the recording.
- They will sing the words along with the singer when they come to the Melody Car.
- Pause recording after vocalist sings one chorus of the song.
- Advise that they will next hear the vocalist scat sing, and then they will hear an instrumentalist improvising their own melody, which is called a solo. While listening to this portion of the recording, they should trace the scat singing and solo in the listening map's Solo Car, moving their finger 'round-and-'round until the soloist finishes. (We want them to try to sense the end of a solo, and wind up at the end of the solo car when each recorded solo is done. Since the instrumental solo is improvised, and children make up the route they take to get to the end of the solo car while listening to the recorded solo, they are also improvising to a certain extent.)
- Release the pause and continue playing CD1-Track 21 to the end.
- Tap "!'s" on the listening map when you hear repeated chords (Fun Car).
- Six phrases: trace with finger moving downward (Happy Car).
- Sing softly the second half of the melody when it is played again (Melody Car).
- Sing softest on the last 2 lines.

Other recommended recordings that children will enjoy:

Duke Ellington, *Blues in Orbit* (Columbia CK 44051). Lots of great blues including the classic "C Jam Blues."
Duke Ellington, *Three Suites* (Columbia CK 46825). This CD includes Ellington/Strayhorn arrangements of Tchaikovsky's *Nutcracker Suite* and Grieg's *Peer Gynt Suites*. It is interesting to compare the Ellington/Strayhorn jazz arrangements of such works as "In the Hall of the Mountain King" to the symphonic originals.

Link to Literature

Duke Ellington

Read aloud *Duke Ellington*, Andrea Davis Pinkney, illustrated by Brian Pinkney (Hyperion).

Optional: Read along to recordings included on *Ken Burns Jazz: The Story of America's Music,* Disc 1, beginning with "East St. Louis Toodle-O," continuing with "Black Beauty" and ending with "Mood Indigo."

Discuss with questions such as:
"What were some of Duke's musicians' names?"

Sonny Greer, Joe "Tricky Sam" Nanton, Otto "Toby" Hardwick, James "Bubber" Miley

"Do you remember what instruments they played?"

Drums, trombone, saxophone, trumpet

"Do you remember some of the dance names that were performed while the Duke Ellington Orchestra played at the Cotton Club?"

Black Bottom, the Fish-Tail, and the Suzy-Q

Bring on the Beat

Read aloud *Bring on the Beat* by Rachel Isadora, G.P. Putnam's Sons (2002). The setting is Harlem in the 1930s. A jazz trio starts playing under a streetlamp. People come out to listen and dance. Riffs of jazz slang sprinkle the wonderfully illustrated pages.
Optional: Read along to a recording of "Cottontail" included on *Ken Burns Jazz: The Story of America's Music,* Disc 3.

Link to History
Websites:

MENC: Duke Ellington website
Go to the MENC web site to have children interact with their Duke Ellington web site for children.
www.MENC.org/news/mag/news.html

A Great Day in Harlem
Another great website about a famous 1958 photograph of jazz musicians in Harlem. To learn about each individual, click on their photo.
www.harlem.org

Ken Burns Jazz Kids
The section "Now and Then" has a good biography on Duke Ellington.
http://www.pbs.org/jazz/kids/nowthen/duke.html

Beyond Category: Duke Ellington Education Kit
This kit has great resources for teaching Duke Ellington. Included in the kit are recordings, overhead transparencies that show art from the Harlem Renaissance, newspapers from the twenties and thirties, pictures of Duke Ellington and his band and a teacher's book with lesson ideas. Dale Seymour Publications/Smithsonian.
www.pearsonlearning.com

Duke Ellington Orchestra: at the Cotton Club
Review archival film clip of the Duke Ellington Orchestra performing at the Cotton Club, Episode 3, *Jazz: A Film by Ken Burns* (PBS Home Video) and excerpt a portion that is suitable for your class.
www.pbs.org/jazz

Link to Cross-Curricular Units: The Harlem Renaissance

Elementary students:

Develop a cross-curricular unit about the Harlem Renaissance for use with elementary classroom teachers.

Language Arts and Social Studies teachers may choose from many wonderful children's books to explore some of Duke Ellington's contemporaries in Harlem that were creating art, poetry, dance and music. For example, Langston Hughes wrote many great poems that link Harlem and jazz together in a rich, rhythmic style.

Read poetry from *The Block,* poems by Langston Hughes and collage by Romare Bearden. New York: Viking, 1995.

Another wonderful book is *Harlem,* poem by Walter Dean Myers and pictures by Christopher Myers. New York: Scholastic Press, 1997.

Watch video clip about Duke Ellington and the Harlem Renaissance on Episode 2, *Jazz: A Film by Ken Burns* (PBS Home Video), about 12 minutes from the beginning. Also featured is a poem by Langston Hughes, plus information about stride piano, rent parties and Ellington's arrival in Harlem. Episode 3 features information about Ellington composing *Black and Tan Fantasy.*

Intermediate students:

Play a recording of Duke Ellington's *Black, Brown and Beige* and lead students to discuss how the mood of the music fits with the experience of African-Americans during slavery and the Civil Rights era.

Cross-Curricular Teacher Resources

Uptown, Brian Collier. New York: Henry Holt and Company, 2000.

Langston Hughes, American Poet, Alice Walker, with paintings by Catherine Deeter. Harper Collins, 2002.

Visiting Langston, Willie Perdomo, illustrated by Bryan Collier. New York: Henry Holt and Company, 2002.

Love to Langston, Tony Medina, illustrated by R. Gregory Christie. New York: Lee & Low Books Inc., 2002.

The Harlem Renaissance, Veronica Chambers. Philadelphia: Chelsea House, 1998.

My Own Harlem, Pellom McDaniels III. Kansas City: Addax Publishing Group, 1998.

Communicating in Jazz

- Call and Response
- Improvisation
- Swing Eighth Notes

Preparing for Success

✓ Jam Session

Students will learn that jazz musicians communicate feelings through their music, and will learn to communicate their own feelings spontaneously through jazz. Students will use call-and-response in chants and while playing instruments. Students will increase their jazz "chops" through singing, chanting and playing.

Activity 1: Jazzy Conversations (Aunt Nora)
Activity 2: Breakfast (Improvisation intro)
Activity 3: Lunch
Activity 4: Dinner
Activity 5: *Poppity Pop Panic*
Activity 6: Mystery Word Game
Link: Mary Lou Williams

Vocabulary

Feelings, communication, melody, spontaneous, improvisation, solo, swing eighth notes

Materials

- *Chop-Monster Jr.* CD1-Track 1 and CD1-Tracks 22–27
- Worksheet 3: Jazz performers
- Mallet (to be used as a pretend microphone)
- Un-pitched rhythm instruments such as rhythm sticks, woodblock, temple block, hand drum (avoid instruments that sustain sound)
- Ride cymbal with drumstick
- F Boomwhacker (short/high)
- C Boomwhacker (long/low)

Indicators of Success

Students are comfortable with call-and-response and can create short answers to questions through rhythmic speech and playing instruments. Students are showing assimilation of jazz skills from previous lessons and communicating feelings through jazz.

♪ Concert Time

Students will demonstrate their understanding of swing eighth notes and call-and-response through independent performance of *Poppity Pop Panic*.

�»　Sitting In

Students will learn about jazz composer and pianist Mary Lou Williams through suggested learning links and listen to her communicative musical style.

Unless specified, you will need to supply your own audio or video recordings.

Link to Jazz Masters

"Scratchin' in the Gravel," Mary Lou Williams. Andy Kirk and Mary Lou Williams, *Mary's Idea.* Decca GRD-622, audio recording.
www.vervemusicgroup.com

"The Lady Who Swings the Band" Sammy Cahn, Saul Chaplin. Andy Kirk and Mary Lou Williams, *Mary's Idea.* Decca GRD-622, audio recording.
www.vervemusicgroup.com

Link to Literature

Willie Jerome, Alice Faye Duncan, illustrated by Tyrone Geter. New York: Atheneum, 1995.

Link to History

Duke University: Mary Lou Williams Jazz Page
http://www.duke.edu/~lmr/

Mary Lou Williams's Salon, photograph by William P. Gottlieb
http://www.jazzphotos.com/marylou.htm

Kennedy Center: Mary Lou Williams Web Site
http://www.kennedycenter.com/programs/jazz/womeninjazz/1st lady.html

✓ Jam Session

Introduction

Swinging Piano Conversations (listening)

"So far we have learned about swing feel but there are other very important parts of jazz: **melody** *and* **improvisation***. Who knows what improvisation means?"*

> Students should be able to identify improvisation as being melody that is composed on the spot.
> Play CD1-Track 1 and have students identify when the melody is played and when the improvisation begins.

"We are going to learn how to improvise in the jazz style. Let's begin with call-and-response. Does anyone remember what call-and-response is?"

Call-and-response was introduced in Unit 1/Part 2 in *That's Jazz!*
Students should remember your call "Marching, Marching" and they responded with "Not Jazz."
Repeat Activity 2 from Unit 1/Part 2 if students need a refresher.

Activity 1 / Jazzy Conversations
Practice Aunt Nora's questions with CD1-Track 22 before teaching this activity.

"We're going to do some call-and-response with a story called "Aunt Nora Comes to Visit."

Step 1:

> Read aloud the "Aunt Nora Comes to Visit" story below.

Aunt Nora Comes to Visit

> Aunt Nora is Sarah's least favorite aunt. Why? Because whenever Aunt Nora comes to visit she asks a lot of nosey questions that Sarah would rather not answer.
>
> Sarah has learned to anticipate Aunt Nora's usual questions and has her answers ready so she can answer them quickly and get back to playing with her cousin Patty.

Step 2:

"Can you guess some questions Aunt Nora might ask Sarah?"

> Mentally note students' suggestions and incorporate them into this activity.

"Here are some other questions Aunt Nora might ask:"

> **"What grade are you in now?"**
> **"How do you like your teacher?"**
> **"What is your favorite school subject?"**
> **"You are really getting big—how old are you again?"**

"What other questions might nosey Aunt Nora ask?"

> Again, make note of students' ideas.

Step 3:

"Be ready for your question from Aunt Nora. You can't be sure which one she will ask, but you need to be quick with your answer or you will be stuck sitting with her on the couch all day! Aunt Nora might be nosey, but she can ask questions with a great swinging feel."

Aunt Nora Comes to Visit

Model how you will ask the questions: Using a mallet as a pretend microphone, ask one student an "Aunt Nora question" in speech, with swing feel.
Extend the pretend microphone toward the student for their answer.

Step 4:

Using CD1-Track 22 to help you "call" and each student "respond" with a good swing feel, ask each student an Aunt Nora question (randomly mixing in your own questions). Continue using the mallet as a pretend microphone.

Step 5:

"Did you know the question you were going to be asked before *I asked it?"*

Students will say no.
Congratulate them on their very imaginative and swinging responses.
"This is how jazz **improvisation** *works: you aren't sure what the questions and answers will be, but you have an idea about the kinds of questions you will be asked. Jazz music is special and different every time it is performed because the musicians* **improvise**.*"*

Activity 2 / Breakfast
Step 1:

"I have two questions about food that I might ask you. I want you to think of ways you can improvise an answer to my question, making your answer sound jazzy. Here are the questions:

"What did you have for breakfast today?" or

"What's your favorite food?"

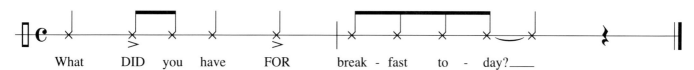

Breakfast,
Performance Model, with lyrics (also models Lunch/Activity 3)

Breakfast,
Backing Track

Step 2:

"Let me show you how this works."

> Use CD1-Track 23 to model pre-recorded questions and answers, or use CD1-Track 24 to model your own questions and answers. Make sure you are using rhythms that reinforce "doodle-dah" triplet subdivision or "doo-dah" swing eighth notes.

Example:

QUESTION: "What's your favorite food?"
ANSWER: see possible answers below

Cer-e-al, cer-e-al, cer-e-al, cer-e-al [doodle-dah]
Mac-n-cheese, mac-n-cheese, mac-n-cheese,
    mac-n-cheese [doodle-dah]
Oat-meal, oat-meal, oat-meal, oat-meal [doo-dah]
Piz-za, piz-za, piz-za, piz-za [doo-dah]
Ta-co, ta-co, ta-co, ta-co [doo-dah]
Sa-lad, sa-lad, sa-lad, sa-lad [doo-dah]

Grand-ma's cook-ing, Grand-ma's cook-ing [doo-dah]
Ice-cream, ice-cream, ice-cream, ice-cream [doo-dah]
Rice-rice, rice-rice, rice-rice, rice-rice (doo-dah)
Eggs and ba-con, eggs and ba-con [doo-dah, doo-dah]
Rice-and-beans, rice-and-beans [doo-dah, doo]
Gum, bub-ble gum, bub-ble gum [doo, doo-dah, doo]

CD-1 Track 24

Breakfast,
Backing Track

Step 3:

- Using backing track CD1-Track 24, take turns asking each student a "breakfast" or "favorite food" question and have them improvise an answer.
- Again, use a mallet as a microphone and point it toward the student who you want to answer so they may speak into it.
- You can also seat the children in a circle and have them pass the mallet to the next person.

Tip from Margaret

Encourage students to be supportive of each other as they improvise (e.g., clap after each solo and make encouraging remarks after each solo) and to try new ideas. The atmosphere of your classroom should reflect "supportive community" while students are learning new concepts. This is a vital component to mastering the singing and playing concepts presented in *Chop-Monster Jr.*

Activity 3 / Lunch

CD-1 Track 24

Backing Track

"This time we are going to try the same thing but we are going to play the answers on rhythm sticks, woodblock or hand drum. I might ask you:

"What did you have for lunch today" or
"What's your favorite food?"—so be ready with an answer!

Use CD1-Track 24.
Sit in circle with children and "ask" one of the two questions by saying and playing the question on un-pitched rhythm instruments (or body percussion).
Go around the circle and have each student play their answer.
Students should be playing the rhythms of their answers on the instruments.

Extension:
Try asking questions on an instrument without using words.
See if the other students can guess what the answers are.

Activity 4 / Dinner

CD-1 Track 25

Dinner,
Performance Model

CD-1 Track 7

Dinner,
Backing Track (same as *Jazzy Band*)

"Now we're going to have a dinner conversation. I'm going to begin by asking a question on one instrument, and you will take turns responding on a different instrument."

Step 1:

- Play CD1-Track 25 to model activity, if desired.
- Sit with class on the floor in a circle.
- Use a long C Boomwhacker for your question (e.g., "What's your favorite food?") and have students pass a short F Boomwhacker and tap the Boomwhacker horizontally for their answers (e.g., "Enchilada, enchilada").
- Hand drums, rhythm sticks, woodblocks or tambourines may be substituted.
- Body percussion may also be used.

Step 2:

"Now we're going to get our swing groove going again."

Dinner,
Backing Track

- Class should remain seated in a circle.
- Hand the C and F Boomwhackers to two students who are sitting directly across from each other in the circle.
- Using backing track, CD1-Track 7, have students pass both C and F Boomwhackers around the circle on beats 2 & 4 (similar to *Jazzy Band,* Unit 1/Activity 5). Whisper doodle-dah triplet subdivision if students need help locking into the swing feel.

Step 3:

"Let's pass the Boomwhackers around our circle again, but this time I will cue you to stop passing, much like when you play musical chairs. The person holding the long C Boomwhacker will ask and play a question and the person holding the short F Boomwhacker opposite them will answer. You will have plenty of time to ask and answer the musical questions, so take your time."

Dinner,
Performance Model

Dinner,
Backing Track

- By positioning the two Boomwhackers directly across the circle, students can make eye contact and know when to play their answers.
- Use performance track CD1-Track 25 to model this activity for students, if desired.
- Use backing track CD1-Track 7. Count off the passing:
  "one, TWO, three, FOUR, one, TWO, three, PASS."
- To cue the C Boomwhacker question, say
  "Stop, TWO, three, FOUR, one, TWO, question, NOW"
- Student who is holding the large C Boomwhacker or other instrument plays a question in two bars. *"What did you have for dinner last night?"*

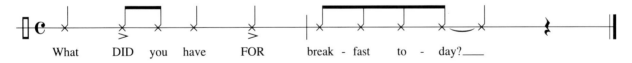

Student with short F Boomwhacker or other instrument answers in 2 bars.
Student plays rhythm of the foods they ate using rhythm of the speech like, "Sal-ad, sal-ad, sal-ad, sal-ad" or "Mac-n-cheese, mac-n-cheese."

Summarize with the idea that in jazz, such improvised playing is called **soloing**. Jazz musicians love to solo because they can express their own ideas and feelings. Your students are learning the first steps in becoming independent music makers, where they can express their thoughts musically from within.

Tip from Kim

When students are comfortable with this activity it is time to go to the next activity. This may take more than one class meeting. Younger children may have trouble at first with stopping and soloing, but they should catch on quickly.

♪ Concert Time

Activity 5 / *Poppity Pop Panic*

Notation for complete song is at the end of this section, which is for teacher reference only. Teach by rote.

*"We're going to learn a song called **Poppity Pop Panic**. What do you think the song is about?"*

Step 1:

- Stand in circle with children and do Chop-Monster Groove, at a slow tempo.
- Chant doodle-dah rhythm, and transition students to ghosting the second note of the triplet ("-dle") so they are chanting "doo-dah, doo-dah" while feeling the triplet subdivision.
- Split class in half if necessary, with one half singing "doodle-dah" and the second half singing "doo-dah." Then switch groups. This will prepare students to chant the swing eighth notes in *Poppity Pop Panic.*
- To assess if students are independent on this activity, have students begin again and then switch parts when you cue them. To cue, say "1, (snap), 2, (snap), 1, 2, 3, switch."

Doodle-dah triplet subdivision (undertow) to swing eighth notes:

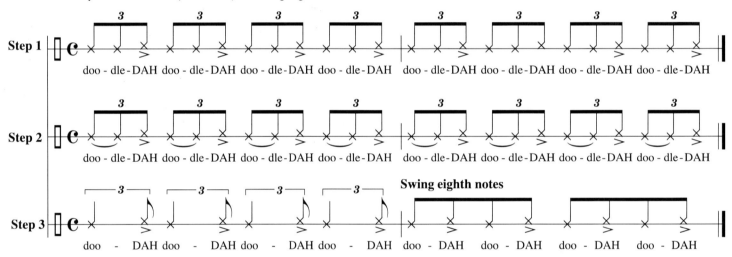

 Poppity Pop Panic, Performance Model
(Twice as written, then with cymbal call-and-response, ending with canon model)

 Poppity Pop Panic,
Backing Track (drummer)

Step 2:

- If desired, model *Poppity Pop Panic* using CD1-Track 26.
- Do Chop-Monster Groove throughout this entire activity.
- Use backing track CD1-Track 27 to demonstrate how the chant sounds with a jazz drummer.
- Without the CD, chant the first two measures of *Poppity Pop Panic* repeatedly, and have children join in.
- When students have memorized the words and can chant on their own, move to Step 3.

Step 3:

"Now we're going to HEAT and SHAKE!"

- Continue CD1-Track 27 and model measures 3 and 4, with pick-up. If you remember the words *heat, shake* and *fast* as key words, it is easy to memorize.
- Continue Chop-Monster Groove.

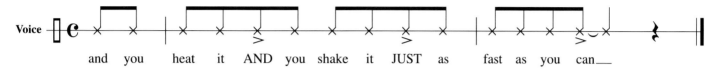

- Invite students to join in the chant. They should swing the eighth notes, feeling the triplet subdivision internally. Observe how well they can perform these measures on their own.
- Chant "doodle-dah" if they have not fully locked in to the subdivision.

Step 4:

Using CD1-Track 27, chant all four measures and repeat until students are swinging.

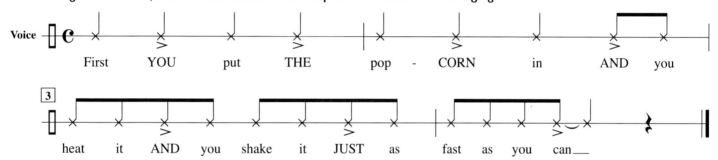

Step 5:

Using CD1-Track 27, teach measures 5–8, keeping accented quarter notes short and crisp.

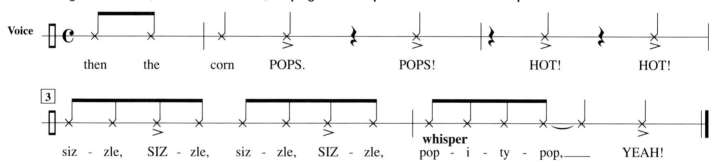

Step 6:

Using CD1-Track 27, put the entire chant together. Repeat as many times as you wish.

Step 7: Add movement

"Now I will select a few students to get in the middle of our circle and pretend to be popcorn. The popcorn people will improvise how high they will pop to beats 2 & 4, during the part of the song where the corn pops. The circle people are the pot and our chanting is the heat."

- Use backing track CD1 Track 27.
- Assign a small group of students to crouch in the middle of the circle during the first four measures while the circle chants. When they hear the words, "then the corn pops–pops–hot!–hot!" (measures 5 and 6), they jump up on beats 2 & 4 from the crouched position. They can choose to jump a short height, a medium height, or to jump high–it's their choice.
- However, since they are swinging kernels, they only pop on beats 2 & 4.
- Optional: additionally, the popcorn people can improvise free movement (move any way they want) during the last two measures.

Step 8: Call-and-response

"We're going to try some call-and-response to this song. When we get to the 'sizzle, sizzle' part of the song, I will 'call' a swinging phrase on the ride cymbal. You will each take a turn echoing my part on a different instrument that will be passed around your circle."

- Teacher stands with a ride cymbal in the middle of the circle for "call."
- Students take turns echoing with rhythm sticks (or a woodblock or temple block with mallet) around circle.
- Chant song to CD1-Track 27.
- At measure 7 (sizzle, sizzle), "call" a swinging rhythm on the ride cymbal for one measure. Examples:

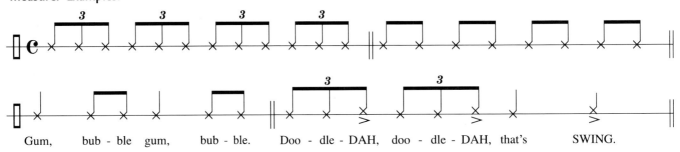

Gum,   bub - ble gum,   bub - ble.   Doo - dle - DAH, doo - dle - DAH, that's   SWING.

- At measure 8, a student in the circle echoes your rhythm exactly.
- As the chant starts over, student passes instrument to the next person.
- Optional: have student improvise a different answer to your call.

Step 9: Teach as a canon

CD-1 Track 26

Poppity Pop Panic,
Performance Model

CD-1 Track 27

Poppity Pop Panic,
Backing Track

Cue CD to the canon portion of CD1-Track 26 (toward the end).
Listen to CD1-Track 26 with the chant performed in canon two times through.
Perform chant in canon two times through with backing track CD1-Track 27.
Canon entry point is measure 3.
Do not use ride cymbal call-and-response for this canon adaptation.
Optional: older students may enjoy the challenge of adding movement with two groups of popcorn people, moving differently to the two different canon parts.

Tip from Kim

You should begin to observe your students integrating swing feel with the doodle-dah undertow. Their call-and-response activities should show that they have assimilated the swing feel from Unit 1 and are now doing it naturally. They should be comfortable finding beats 2 & 4 and you will notice them bobbing their heads to beats 2 & 4 as they listen, sing or play. If they have trouble consistently doing these activities with good swing feel then review activities from Unit 1.

Canon begins at measure 3.

Poppity Pop Panic

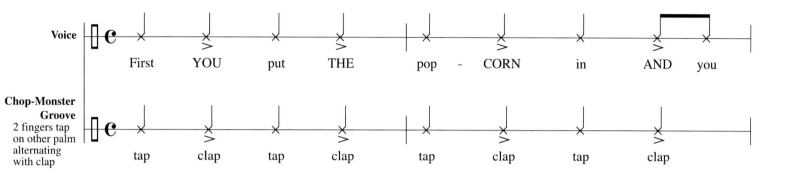

Voice — First YOU put THE pop - CORN in AND you

Chop-Monster Groove
2 fingers tap on other palm alternating with clap — tap clap tap clap tap clap tap clap

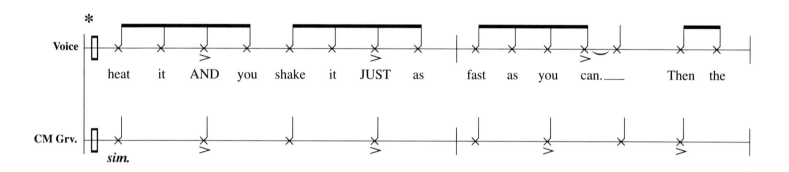

Voice — heat it AND you shake it JUST as fast as you can.___ Then the

CM Grv. — *sim.*

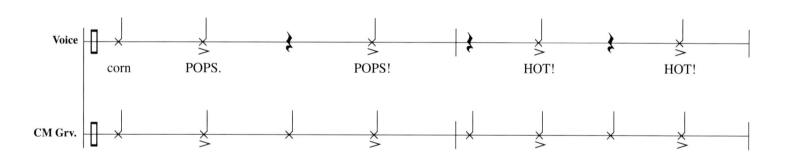

Voice — corn POPS. POPS! HOT! HOT!

CM Grv.

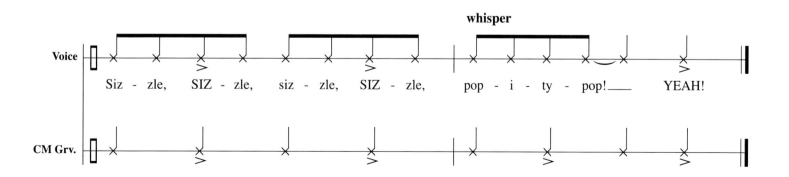

whisper

Voice — Siz - zle, SIZ - zle, siz - zle, SIZ - zle, pop - i - ty - pop!___ YEAH!

CM Grv.

Activity 6 / Mystery Word Game

*"This game begins with words in certain categories that are spoken and sung in rhythm, and adjectives that describe the words. We'll end the game taking turns playing the rhythms of **mystery** words, and the class will try to guess what those mystery words are."*

CD-1
Track 24

Mystery Word Game
(Backing Track only; same as "Breakfast/Lunch")

Step 1:

Select a word category from below and model several words and adjectives for students, using swinging rhythms. For example, from the animal category listed below, select the word "chimps" and match it with an adjective such as chattering: "chat-ter-ing chimps." You should feel free to customize this game to suit your classroom.

Chat - ter - ing CHIMPS

Mystery Game Word Categories and Adjectives

Colors	Animals	Sports	Food
Sun-shin-y yel-low	Chat-ter-ing chimps	Slip-pit-y soc-cer	Goo-ey fudge
Mid-night blue	Cud-dly Ko-a-la	Jig-gling gym-nas-tics, sen-sa-tion-al som-er-saults	Chew-y gum
Choc-o-late brown	Roar-ing lion		Spic-y nachos
Squirt-y o-range	Slink-y snake	Bone-crush-ing foot-ball	Ten-der chick-en nug-gets
Ghost-ly grey	Hap-py-hop-py toad	Slam-ming bas-ket-ball	Stick-y, stuck-y, P, B & J (peanut butter and jelly)
		Hot-dog-ging snow-board-ing	

Step 2:

- Have in mind one word category to begin the game (e.g., animals). Limit your choice to four different category words. For example, chimps, koala, lion and snake. Also have some adjectives ready to suggest: chattering, cuddly, roaring, slinky, etc. We've provided a few examples to get you started.
- Group students in pairs for the first part of this activity. Each pair needs to come up with one word from the category and one describing word to go with it. For example, in the animal category: chimps and chattering = "chattering chimps" (doodle-dah, doo).
- Give students 45 seconds or so to decide on their category word and a describing adjective.

Step 3:

- Ask students to sit in a circle next to their partner.
- Go around the circle and have partners share their word groupings with everyone else.
- Pick *one* example from the group to teach the game.
- Give pairs 45 seconds or so to come up with a special way to say the selected word grouping in a jazz style (for example, on beats 2 & 4, with doodle-dah or swing eighths rhythms, a ride-cymbal pattern).
- Play CD1-Track 24 while they are doing this and instruct them to make the words "fit" with the track. If they can easily fit the words with the jazz backing track, they are well on their way with internalizing the jazz "language."

Step 4:

Play CD1-Track 24 again. Using a pretend microphone, go around the circle prompting the pairs to chant or sing together their version of the selected word/adjective by asking:

"What did you do to your words today?"

Say this in a swing style as you go around the circle, pointing to the next pair as you say the prompt. Everyone should have a way to say the selected word grouping (e.g., "Chattering Chimps").

Step 5: Try It on Your Own

- This time, let the pairs chose their *own* word plus a describing word from the class's word category.
- Instruct them to experiment with their partners with the rhythm of the words until they think the phrase sounds "jazzy." They should say the words 4 times in a pattern, and be ready to chant their pattern to the CD track.
- Give them a set time limit to do this experimentation.

Step 6:

- Play CD1-Track 24.
- Go around the circle as before with your verbal prompt.
- The goal is to elicit a response featuring jazz elements, chanted in time to the recording.
- Use praise to motivate! If you hear a wonderful response, respond afterward like a jazz audience and say, "yeah!"
- At this point, they are likely to be uncomfortable with being "out in the open" with their ideas. This is to be expected. Your role is to scaffold the kids to a comfort level with improvisation and to raise their skills to the next level.

Step 7:

"Now comes the Mystery Word portion of the game!"

- Ask the pairs to come up with a *different* word that fits with your word category of the day, and a different *describing* word.
- Instruct them to again experiment with the rhythm of the words until they think the phrase sounds "jazzy." However, when performing this time, the pairs will not say the category word because it is a **mystery**. They will do body percussion or sing with scat syllables for their mystery word instead. For example, if the word category is food, and they select ice cream for their mystery word, and "choc-o-late" or "cream-y" for their describing word, they would sing something like "choc-o-late doo-dah" or "cream-y doo-dah."
- Allow pairs time to practice, keeping the CD going while they are working quietly. Go around and monitor progress, but try not to make suggestions.

Step 8:

- Play CD1-Track 24 again.
- Pairs will perform their describing word and their mystery word 4 times in a pattern, and be ready to perform their pattern to the CD track.
- Pause the recording after each pair performs their pattern.
- Class will evaluate each pair's performance with the following "quality control" questions, holding up one finger for "yes," and two fingers for "no."

"Did the performance sound like jazz?"
"Was the choice of words interesting to listen to?"
"Did you figure out the mystery word?"

Let the class guess the mystery word, and pairs confirm the word.

- You can also ask guiding questions as suggested in the Introduction to pull out appropriate responses to your questions.
- The goal with this last step is to guide students to helpful, meaningful critiques of peers that reflect their understanding of jazz style. Hopefully this will lead them to have a better understanding of how to build jazz "responses" that are interesting musically. This is an important step towards purposeful improvisation! Use lots of praise where deserved and don't be afraid to record the finished product for the entire class to evaluate.

Tip from Margaret

It is great to make recordings of your class performances as you go along. Then you can play back the recordings and students can hear how they have grown as jazz improvisers. Have them compare Jazz-Ma-Tazz to the Mystery Word Game. They should hear themselves being more expressive. These recordings can be put in a professional portfolio to demonstrate to administrators your progress as a teacher with your students. You can also create portfolios for individual students as well.

⊙ Sitting In

The following activities reference resources that are not included with *Chop-Monster Jr.,* such as audio and video recordings and children's literature. We offer these lesson-enrichment ideas to help increase student awareness about the lives and contributions of the great jazz masters.

Link to Jazz Masters: Learning with Mary Lou Williams

Courtesy of the Institute of Jazz Studies

Mary Lou Williams

Mary Lou Williams (1910–1981)

"Mary Lou Williams was born in 1910. She was a pianist, composer and a great jazz musician. In 1931 Mary Lou joined a Kansas City band, Andy Kirk and his Twelve Clouds of Joy, and quickly became the star of the band. She wrote most of the music for the band. She also arranged music for other famous bands such as those led by pianist Duke Ellington and clarinetist Benny Goodman. She moved to New York City and many younger musicians used to go to her apartment in Harlem to get pointers and lessons from her. Some of the people who hung out at Mary Lou's were pianists Thelonious Monk and Bud Powell, and trumpet player, Dizzy Gillespie. She was one of the first jazz composers to write music for a classical symphony orchestra when the New York Philharmonic played her *Zodiac Suite* at Carnegie Hall in 1945 in New York City."

Reproducible Worksheet/Transparency Master 3: Jazz Performers

Display a transparency made from Worksheet 3 and identify Mary Lou Williams.
Or go to photographer William P. Gottlieb's website to see a photo of musicians at Mary Lou Williams's apartment.
http://www.jazzphotos.com/marylou.htm

Learning with Mary Lou Williams

Listening: Scratchin' in the Gravel

Locate a recording of "Scratchin' in the Gravel" by Mary Lou Williams (Decca). Listen to her play " Scratchin' in the Gravel" and hear the doodle-dah rhythms. See if students can perform the kneedle-dah when they hear the doodle-dah played on the recording.

Encourage discussion about the type of feelings your students feel the music communicates, and why Mary Lou Williams might have titled the work "Scratchin' in the Gravel."

Extension: The Lady Who Swings the Band

- Locate a recording of "The Lady Who Swings the Band" for a song that tells all about the great Mary Lou (Decca).

- Ask students to create a list of questions and answers based on what they learned about Mary Lou from the recording. For example, "In what town did Mary Lou play music?" (The recording says, "Kansas City's Mary Lou.")

- Use CD1-Track 7 and play the "Dinner" game again, but call-and-response is now based on questions and answers learned about Mary Lou. After you call the question, each student will say their answer and simultaneously play the same rhythm on the Boomwacker.

Link to Literature

Willie Jerome

Read aloud *Willie Jerome* by Alice Faye Duncan, illustrated by Tyrone Geter (Athaneum).

Optional: Read along to recordings featured on the compact disc, Andy Kirk and Mary Lou Williams, *Mary's Idea* (Decca GRD-622), beginning with "Mary's Idea," continuing through "Close to Five" and finishing with "Scratchin' in the Gravel."

"In this book, Willie Jerome is learning to play jazz trumpet and everyone in the neighborhood except his sister thinks he sounds like noise. When you are learning to be a jazz musician and a composer like Mary Lou Williams it takes lots of practice to become really good. This is a great story about how the first few years of practicing can be frustrating for beginners and the people who listen to them. We all need time to develop into jazz musicians and teachers like me are there to help you. Teachers are important to beginning jazz musicians. Mary Lou loved to help teach young people about jazz."

Link to History
Websites:

Ken Burns Jazz
Mary Lou Williams biography.
www.pbs.org/jazz/biography/artist_id_williams_mary_lou.htm

Duke University: Mary Lou Williams Jazz Page
www.duke.edu/~lmr/

Mary Lou Williams's Salon
www.jazzphotos.com/marylou.htm

Kennedy Center: Mary Lou Williams Website
www.kennedycenter.com/programs/jazz/womeninjazz/1stlady.html

NPR's Jazz Profiles: Mary Lou Williams
Host Nancy Wilson profiles Mary Lou Williams.
www.npr.org/programs/jazzprofiles/archive/williams_m.html

Nancy Wilson's profile of Mary Lou Williams is also featured in the Biography section of the website for *Jazz: A Film by Ken Burns.*

Scatting in Jazz

- Scat singing on one pitch
- Self-assessment
- Peer-assessment

Preparing for Success

✅ Jam Session

Students will scat sing on one pitch using varied rhythms and inflection. Through these experiences, students will become more comfortable developing thoughtful and purposeful improvised solos. Students will self-assess and peer assess on the scat improvisations performed in class.

> Activity 1: Scat Singing
> Activity 2: Scat and Groove on One Pitch (*I'm Scattin'*)
> Activity 3: More Scat and Groove on One Pitch
> Activity 4: Scat and Answer on One Pitch
> Activity 5: Self-Assessing/Peer-Assessing
> Activity 6: Thinking About Improvisation
> Activity 7: *Swing That Note!*
> Link: Ella Fitzgerald

Vocabulary

Scat singing, scatting, inflection

Materials

- *Chop-Monster Jr.* CD1-Tracks 28–30 and CD2-Tracks 1–3
- Worksheet 3: Jazz Performers
- Worksheet 7: Thinking About Improvisation
- Worksheet 8: "How High the Moon" Listening Map
- Ride Cymbal with drumstick
- Alto Glockenspiel with 2 mallets (E and A)
- Bass xylophone with 2 mallets (D and G), or D and G Bass Boomwhackers
- Optional: Soprano Recorders (one note: G)

Indicators of Success

Students are successful improvising on one pitch and are reflecting on their improvised solos, and solos performed by their peers.

🎵 Concert Time

Students independently perform the song *Swing That Note!* and scat sing and improvise with one note over an Orff accompaniment vamp.

💿 Sitting In

Students will learn about the development of scat singing and the incredible vocalist Ella Fitzgerald through suggested learning links.

Unless specified, you will need to supply the referenced audio or video recordings.

Link to Jazz Masters

Chop-Monster Jr. CD2-Track 3
"How High the Moon," Nancy Hamilton, Morgan Lewis. Carmen Bradford, Alfred Publishing, audio recording.
www.alfred.com

"How High the Moon," Nancy Hamilton, Morgan Lewis. *Something to Live For,* Ella Fitzgerald, Polygram, audio recording.
www.vervemusicgroup.com

Link to Literature

Ella Fitzgerald, The Tale of a Vocal Virtuosa, Andrea Davis Pinkney and Brian Pinkney. New York: Hyperion Books for Children, 2002.
www.disney.go.com/disneybooks/hyperionbooks

Link to History

Jazz for Young People Curriculum, Lesson 16, Marsalis, New York: Jazz at Lincoln Center, 2002, teaching curriculum with 30 student guides, 10-CD set audio recordings and video recording.
www.jazzatlincolncenter.org

Archival film featuring "A Tisket, A Tasket," performed by Ella Fitzgerald from the feature film *Ride 'Em Cowboy,* 1942, is included in *Jazz: A Film by Ken Burns*, Episode 6, Florentine Films/PBS/Warner Home Video, 10-episode video series (also DVD).
www.pbs.org/jazz

✅ Jam Session

Introduction

*"So far we have created improvised solos using call-and-response and of course we still have that great swing feel in our music. Now we are going to improvise with our singing voices. When singers improvise it is called **scat singing**. When a singer **scats** they improvise using crazy nonsense syllables that aren't words but more like sounds. Some singers like to make their scat solos sound like instruments. The syllables and nonsense words help them to communicate their feelings to their listeners."*

Activity 1 / Scat Singing

CD-1
Track 28

I'm Scattin' (Listening, followed by call-and-response)

"Let's listen to some scat singing. We will hear the melody of the song, interspersed with scat singing."

> Play CD1-Track 28 and fade after "I'm Scattin'" melody/scat singing section, and discuss.

> ### *I'm Scattin'*
> Featuring Tierney Sutton
>
> *Gonna tell you all about my cat,*
>
> *'Cause she's the one who taught me to scat.*
>
> *If you listen, you'll scat, too.*
>
> *[scat . . .]*
>
> *I'm scattin' . . . I'm scattin'*
>
> *Follow me and you'll scat, too!*

Activity 2 / Scat and Groove on One Pitch

"We're going to learn how to scat sing, but we will start very simply. We will scat sing on one pitch, using call-and-response. Let's listen first, and groove."

CD-1
Track 28

Scat and Groove on One Pitch

Step 1:

> Have students listen to CD1-Track 28 while doing the Chop-Monster Groove.

Step 2:

"Now we'll do it again, but this time you will echo the singer on the recording when I cue you. Match the singer's phrasing and mood exactly."

- Play CD1-Track 28 again and continue Chop-Monster Grove.
- Cue students to echo sing after the "I'm Scattin'" introductory section.
- Repeat until students have memorized many of the jazz phrases.
- Listen for how well students are matching the pitch

Tip from Margaret

If your students are mastering the one-note scatting activities quickly, you don't need to repeat them and break them down as much. We encourage you to use the book at the pace that is most comfortable for your students. At this point, children should be able to keep the Chop-Monster Groove while singing. They should also begin to accurately match the one pitch and respond/echo the correct rhythm and vocal inflection as recorded by the singer.

Activity 3 / More Scat and Groove on One Pitch

CD-1
Track 29

More Scat and Groove on One Pitch

This recording organizes the call-and-response into 4-measure increments, which allows extra time for students to reflect on their echo response:

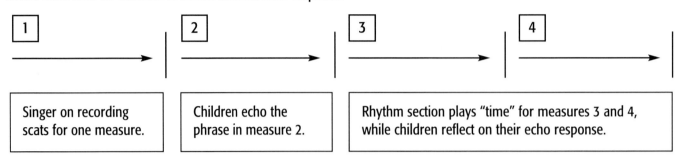

| 1 | 2 | 3 | 4 |

Singer on recording scats for one measure.

Children echo the phrase in measure 2.

Rhythm section plays "time" for measures 3 and 4, while children reflect on their echo response.

Step 1:

Using CD1-Track 29, direct students to do the Chop-Monster Groove while listening only, and ask them to figure out how many measures they do the Chop-Monster Groove in between the times the singer sings (three measures).

Step 2:

- Use CD1-Track 29 again but this time children should echo the singer during the second measure. Continue the Chop-Monster Groove throughout.
- After echoing the singer there is a 2-bar reflection time for students to think about what they just sang, which helps them to build their jazz language.

CD-1
Track 29

Activity 4 / Scat and Answer on One Pitch

Step 1:

- Students sit in a large circle with space between each other.
- Use CD1-Track 29 again. Use the Chop-Monster Groove also.
- Students improvise a 1-bar phrase on one pitch (F) that *answers* the singer's phrase, instead of echoing. However, it is important that they use rhythms/inflections that they previously learned with CD1-Track 28 and CD1-Track 29 so you may hear how well they are internalizing the jazz language.
- *Everyone improvises* at the same time. This provides children with a safe way to try out their ideas.
- As you go around the room, listen for how well they are matching the pitch.
- If children are reluctant to sing out, have them roll a piece of paper into a tube, and sing into the tube as they direct it toward you.

Step 2:

- Use CD1-Track 29 again.
- Before asking your students to improvise again to the recording, explain to children that during the "wait time" after their solo, and during the time that the singer sings again, they should be thinking about what they just sang and then think of a phrase they might try for the next solo.
- Repeat as desired. Remind students again to draw upon musical phrases they've sung previously.
- Ask for one or two individual volunteers/demonstrators if you feel a few of your students are ready. Remind the rest of your class that they are the cheering section!

Activity 5: Self-Assessment and Peer-Assessment Scat Solos

CD-1
Track 29

More Improvising on One Pitch

Step 1: Self-Assessment

- Select a few students to try this self-assessment activity before having the entire class try it. Remind class that they are a supportive community, and that all will eventually take a turn doing the same activity.
- Explain that each "demonstrator" will take turns soloing by themselves during the measure after the singer on the CD. Each soloist will then evaluate their own performance after their improvisation by holding up one finger if they felt their solo sounded like jazz to them, and holding up two fingers if it did not sound like jazz to them.
- Remind soloists that they should sing the same note they were singing as a group, and sing a jazz rhythm they've already learned through call-and-response.
- Use CD1-Track 29 and repeat.

Step 2: Peer-Assessment

CD-1
Track 30

Open Backing Track for One-Note Improvisation

"This time, we're going to take turns improvising to a CD track that does not have the singer. It is a chance for you to take turns soloing for one measure on your one note, with a jazz rhythm section. This time the class will rate the solos by holding up one finger for a solo that sounds like jazz, or two fingers for a solo that does not sound like jazz. I will cue you when it is your turn."

- Again, select a few student "demonstrators" to model this activity before you expand to the entire class.
- Play CD1-Track 30, which is an "open track" and go around the circle, cueing each person with a pretend microphone to scat sing their 1-bar solos, and receive ratings from others in the class.

Activity 6: Thinking About Improvisation

CD-1
Track 29

Worksheet 7: Thinking About Improvisation
(with vocalist)

Step 1:

- Divide the class into groups with four students per group.
- Tell the students they are Vocal Jazz Quartets and they are going to peer-assess each Jazz Quartet's scat solos.

Step 2:

- Each Jazz Quartet will need to decide who will be Singer 1, Singer 2, Singer 3, and Singer 4.
- They will each respond to a call on the CD, so there will be four responses to four calls per Jazz Quartet.

Step 3:

Allow groups to practice singing scat solos with CD1-Track 29 at least once and probably two or three times. They should sing in order by Singer number (i.e., Singer 1 first, Singer 2 second, and so on.)

Step 4:

Distribute Worksheet 7: Thinking About Improvisation Worksheet.

"Here's how this works. If you are a Singer 1, you will evaluate only other Singer 1's solos on your worksheet. If you are a Singer 2, you will evaluate only other Singer 2's. You will mark your assessment on the worksheet. I will pause the track after each Vocal Jazz Quartet improvises to allow time for you to write comments."

Step 5:

- Vocal Jazz Quartets take turns improvising.
- Class listens and completes their worksheets as outlined in Step 4.

Step 6:

- Discuss solos with the group. Ask the 1s to describe the other 1s solos, and so on.
- Use "Guided Questions for Reflecting" (see Introduction).

Step 7:

Have students hand in their worksheets.

Tip From Kim

Be sure to look through the worksheets to see the comments from your students. You may be surprised at how sophisticated some of them are. Share some of the comments in the next class. Reflecting on improvisation helps to build jazz vocabulary. Use the self/peer-assessments often as a way for your students to think deeply about improvisation and as a way for you to check their progress.

Tip From Margaret

The students I meet and work with each year never fail to teach me a great deal. One lesson my students have taught me is to let things "simmer" through the use of reflection. One time I was experimenting with a new improvisation piece and my students asked me guiding questions about why I had written it the way I did—they were great! I learned a lot about musical things that I do in an automatic fashion—and I learned that when we all are given the time to reflect in a meaningful way, we all learn more. Some of my guiding questions may seem simple to you, but please take that few minutes to let your students' brains "simmer" out the answers. The power of their "A-Ha!" moment is a thing of beauty. I've also had the class brainstorm rubrics to reflect upon. It is yet another avenue to check for understanding. See Introduction for "Guided Questions for Reflecting."

Concert Time

Note: Switch to CD-2

Activity 7 / *Swing That Note!*

CD-2 Track 1
Swing That Note!
Performance Model with Call-and-Response

CD-2 Track 2
Swing That Note!
Backing Track

Swing That Note! Room Setup Diagram

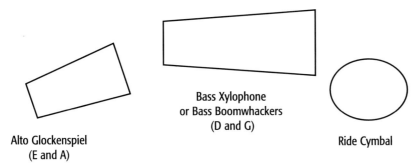

Bass Xylophone
or Bass Boomwhackers
(D and G)

Ride Cymbal

Alto Glockenspiel
(E and A)

Optional: Recorders (one note, G)

The arrangement of *Swing That Note!* offers a variety of performance options, and will demonstrate to students how much they have learned about jazz. They are swinging on the ride cymbal, they are keeping a steady beat on the bass xylophone or Boomwhackers, they are singing with swinging rhythms and inflection, and they are scat singing their creative ideas on one note.

Step 1: *Call-and-Response*

- Use CD2-Track 1 to model the song *Swing That Note!* This track also features a one note call-and-response section. (When students perform the piece on their own with backing track CD2-Track 2, the call-and-response section becomes the solo section).
- When CD2-Track 1 gets to the call-and-response section, children echo the singer's calls on one note (G). Repeat as needed until they are imitating exactly the singer's inflections.
- Optional: have children echo by playing recorders on one note (G).

Step 2: *Teach Melody*

- Teach both verses of the melody by rote.
- Children should do the Chop-Monster Groove throughout.
- If your piano chops are in good shape, have fun accompanying your students using the written piano part. If you do not want to play piano, use backing track CD2-Track 2 for the final performance. If you do not want to use the backing track, simply have students sing the melody a cappella along with the ride cymbal.
- Have a few students take turns playing the ride cymbal part.

Melody:

You may think that grown - ups_ are hav - in' all the fun,__ but,
Now you know why par - ents_ are wish - in' they were small:_

[5]

while they're in the of - fice,__ we're out in the sun.__
run - nin' round the play - ground, throw - in' 'round the ball.__

[9]

We can't watch the late__ show_ and we can't e - ven vote,__ but,
We can't watch the late__ show_ and we don't get to vote,__ but,

[13]

there's one thing_ we can__ do:__ Swing that note!
there's one thing_ we can__ do:__ Swing that note!

Step 3: Teach Solo Section Orff Accompaniment

- Set up Orff instruments as shown in the *Swing That Note!* Room Setup Diagram.
- Continue ride cymbal part and Chop-Monster Groove.
- Teach Orff parts (bass xylophone and alto xylophone) by rote. These parts create a very simple background groove for the "solo section." Try to give everyone a turn, if practical.

Step 4: Improvise

- While Orff instruments and ride cymbal repeat their accompaniment pattern, the rest of the students take a turn scat singing solos on one note (G) using rhythms they learned in the call-and-response section. Have children pass a pretend microphone down the line while they scat sing their 2-bar solos. Leave 2 bars of "time" between each soloist for reflection.
- Optional: students play recorders to improvise on one note (G).

Step 5: Putting It All Together

- Perform the entire piece, repeating the solo section as many times as needed for everyone to *swing* that note!

Swing That Note

You may think that grown - ups__ are hav - in' all the fun,__ but,

Now you know why par - ents__ are wish - in' they were small:__

⊙ Sitting In

The following activities reference resources that are not included with *Chop-Monster Jr.,* such as audio and video recordings and children's literature. We offer these lesson-enrichment ideas to help increase student awareness about the lives and contributions of the great jazz masters.

Link to Jazz Masters: Scatting with Ella Fitzgerald

Ella Fitzgerald (1917–1996)

"Ella Fitzgerald was born in 1917. She was one of the greatest jazz singers ever. Ella listened to horn players and used horn-like sounds in her scat solos. She took ideas from listening to Louis Armstrong scat sing and used them to create her own style. Musicians loved to perform with Ella because she always sang in tune and sang great scat solos. Ella Fitzgerald is still listened to by those who want to become great jazz singers. We are going to listen to Ella scat sing on one of her most famous recordings called 'How High the Moon.'

"Ella originally dreamed about being a dancer and entered an amateur contest at the Apollo Theatre in Harlem. Once she got there and saw the other dancers who performed ahead of her, she realized she would lose the contest based on her dancing abilities. So at the last minute she changed her mind and sang! She was 'discovered' there and soon joined a great jazz band led by drummer Chick Webb. When Chick Webb died, Ella continued to lead the band for many years. She became one of the most beloved jazz singers in the world."

Courtesy of the Institute of Jazz Studies

Ella Fitzgerald

Teacher's Guide to Listening Activity

Scatting with Ella Fitzgerald

Listening: How High the Moon

***Chop-Monster Jr.*: How High the Moon**
Use our recording of "How High the Moon" on CD2-Track 3 featuring Carmen Bradford. (Carmen Bradford sang and toured with Count Basie for nine years.)
Or, locate a recording of "How High the Moon" by Ella Fitzgerald, *Something to Live For* (Verve).

CD-2
Track 3

Review the worksheet before you play "How High the Moon" for students. Be comfortable enough with the song that you are able to tell the students when the following occurs in the tune: Introduction, Verse 1, Verse 2, Verse 3 and Verse 4.

Review Worksheet:

Explain each question, asking for examples from the students.
Review the term *tempo* (speed of the music).

Before playing the tune, explain that Verses 1 and 2 have words, and Verses 3 and 4 are scatted. Explain that there is something *different* about the Verse 2. (After listening, students should be able to identify that the words are improvised in Verse 2.)

Answers:

For Verse 1 and Verse 2, students should identify the instruments playing: rhythm section, trumpets, saxophones, etc., and the balance of the ensemble compared to the singer.

Drum break: TEMPO goes into double time. Students will probably answer that the music "goes faster." That is fine, or you can define as double time for older students.

For Verse 3 and Verse 4, students should write down scat syllables that they hear and like.
A sample answer for the scat question is provided on the worksheet for students.

They should also write comments on Carmen Bradford's or Ella Fitzgerald's vocal style and inflections. Examples: sounds like a trumpet; smooth sound; twisty notes; slides around; etc.

Optional Activity:

CD-1

CD1-Track 30
Play CD1-Track 30 and have students try out their choices of scat syllables! They can scat on one note, or scat rhythmically—whatever you feel is appropriate. This should be fun!

Additional Listening:

Recordings:
There are many great Ella Fitzgerald recordings to which children would respond enthusiastically. Some of our favorites are:

Ella Fitzgerald: Something to Live For
Verve 314547800-2

Ella at Duke's Place
Verve 314529700-2

Ella in Rome: The Birthday Concert
Verve 835 454-2

Link to Literature

Ella Fitzgerald: A Tale of a Vocal Virtuosa
Read aloud *Ella Fitzgerald: A Tale of a Vocal Virtuosa* by Andrea Davis Pinkney, illustrated by Brian Pinkney (Hyperion).

In this book a feline character named Scat Cat Monroe tells Ella's story in an imaginative narrative. The book is organized into four sections: Hoofin' in Harlem, Jammin' at Yale, Stompin' at the Savoy, and Carnegie Hall Scat. A concise biography is included at the end of the book.

Optional: After reading the book, play a recording of "A Tisket, A Tasket" from the compact disc by Ella Fitzgerald, *Something to Live For* (Polygram/Verve, #3145478002).

Link to History

Jazz: A Film by Ken Burns
Show Episode 6 of *Jazz: A Film by Ken Burns* (PBS Home Video) with Ella Fitzgerald singing "A Tisket, A Tasket." Or, watch Episode 8 with Ella Fitzgerald singing "Oh, Lady Be Good."

Jazz for Young People Curriculum
Lesson 16 of the *Jazz for Young People Curriculum* focuses on the history and contributions of jazz vocalists. *Jazz for Young People Curriculum*, Marsalis, New York: Jazz at Lincoln Center, 2002, compact discs/teacher's guide/student guides. www.jazzatlincolncenter.org

Websites:

VH1 Ella Fitzgerald Web Page
Features a longer biography with information about her big band years with Chick Webb plus a discography of recordings she made with other big bands. www.vh1.com/artists/az/fitzgerald_ella/bio.jhtml

The Leonard Feather Scrapbooks
Sound files of Ella interviewed by jazz writer, Leonard Feather are featured along with clips of her singing and a biography. www.leonardfeather.com/feather_26.html

Downbeat Magazine
A short biography and several pictures of Ella through her life. www.downbeat.com/artists/window.asp?action=new&aid=185&aname=Ella+Fitzgerald

Ella Fitzgerald 1917–1996
The Great American Songbook Audio website. Sound files of Ella singing and interviews about Ella Fitzgerald are featured on this memorial site. http://museum.media.org/ella/

Improvising in Jazz

- Scat Singing with Two Pitches

- Improvising on Instruments
  with Two Pitches

Preparing for Success

✔ Jam Session

Students will scat sing on two pitches using swing feel. Students will self-assess and peer-assess on scat improvisations.

> Activity 1: Jazzy Sax Plays Two Pitches
> Activity 2: Scat and Groove with Two Pitches
> Activity 3: Scat and Move with Two Pitches
> Activity 4: Scat and Answer with Two Pitches
> Activity 5: *Impro-Wise*
> Activity 6: Improvising on *Impro-Wise*
> Activity 7: Got Chops?
> Link: Count Basie

Vocabulary

community, riff, harmony

Materials

- *Chop-Monster Jr.* CD2-Tracks 4–9
- Worksheet 9: Got Chops?
- Mallet (for pretend microphone)
- Ride Cymbal with drumstick
- Alto glockenspiel with 2 mallets (E and A)
- Bass xylophone with 2 mallets (G and D) or G and D Bass Boomwhackers
- Soprano recorders (optional, two notes: G and B)

Indicators of Success

Students will comfortably improvise 2-bar solos using two pitches. Students can show movements corresponding to pitches. Students give feedback and their reflections show growing sophistication in their understanding of jazz.

♪ Concert Time

Students will demonstrate their ability to scat sing using two notes through the performance of *Impro-Wise*.

∞ Sitting In

Students will learn about Count Basie and His Orchestra and their ability to create swinging jazz charts out of riffs and improvisations through suggested learning links.

Unless specified, you will need to supply the referenced audio or video recordings.

Link to Jazz Masters

"Jumping at the Woodside," William Basie, *Best of Early Basie,* GRP, audio recording. www.vervemusicgroup.com

"Jumping at the Woodside," *Ken Burns Jazz: The Story of America's Music*, Disc 2, Columbia/Legacy 5-CD set (from *The Complete Decca Recordings*, GRP), audio recording. www.legacyrecordings.com

Link to Literature

Who Bop?, Jonathan London, pictures by Henry Cole. New York: HarperCollins Publishers, 2000. www.harperchildrens.com

Link to History

Count Basie and His Orchestra are featured extensively in *Jazz: A Film by Ken Burns,* Episode 6, Florentine Films/PBS/Warner Home Video, video recording (also DVD). www.pbs.org/jazz

Jazz for Young People Curriculum, Lesson 7, Marsalis, New York: Jazz at Lincoln Center, 2002, teaching curriculum with 30 student guides, 10-CD set audio recordings and video recording. www.jazzatlincolncenter.org

✓ Jam Session

Introduction

"Let's think for a minute about all of the things you can use when you improvise. You can groove and use jazzy rhythms like in Jazz-Ma-Tazz and Recess, Yes! You can sing, you can play instruments and you can move. You can do all of this to your solid swing feel. Using these musical elements, you can create great improvised solos that communicate your feelings or moods. Let's continue to develop your jazz language by using two pitches for scat singing. Using another pitch in your solos will allow you more ways to express yourself."

Activity 1 / Jazzy Sax Plays Two Pitches

CD-2
Track 4

Jazzy Sax Plays Two Pitches

"We'll first listen to a recording of a jazz group with saxophone, and hear how the saxophone plays two pitches and jazz rhythms. Then we'll try it with our scat singing!"

> Listen to CD2-Track 4 and discuss.

Activity 2 / Scat and Groove with Two Pitches

CD-2
Track 5

Scat and Groove with call and response

Step 1:

> Play CD2-Track 5 and have students listen to the singer scat on two pitches while doing the Chop-Monster Groove.

Step 2:

- Play CD2-Track 5 again and direct students to echo the singer on the recording. Continue Chop-Monster Groove. During the wait time students should think about what they just sang.
- Repeat several times until students are memorizing the two-note jazz phrases.

Extension:
If you teach recorders in the classroom, repeat Steps 1 through 3, having students play recorders to CD2-Track 5, using the notes G and B.

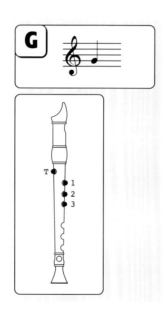

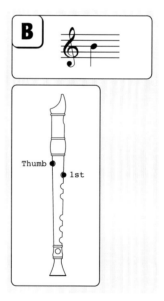

Tip from Margaret

Are you wondering why we did not use sol/mi? The idea behind using the root of the chord is that children, in order to be able to "converse" in the language of jazz authentically need to be able to "hear" the root of the chord. By the time you are teaching your children about jazz, they should have already had experience with sol/mi material. This approach of using the root is not meant to change other activities you may do with your classes, it is to scaffold them to a successful and more meaningful understanding and experience in jazz.

Activity 3: Scat and Move with Two Pitches

CD-2

Track 5

Scat and Groove with Two Pitches

Step 1:

- Skip Step 1 if you are doing this activity directly after Activity 2.
- Students select partners and face each other.
- Play CD2-Track 5 again and direct students to do the Chop-Monster Groove and echo sing.
- On the recording, the singer scats in measure 1, students echo in measure 2, and the rhythm section plays two measures of "time" to give students time to reflect, and so on.

Step 2: Add movement

Partners are facing each other.
Play CD2-Track 5, and direct students to echo sing, but this time also tap waist for the root (do) and shoulders for the 3rd (mi). The movements should occur on the echo using rhythms of singer's call. Partners will mirror each other.

Step 3: Optional

Play CD2-Track 4 again (featuring the saxophone), and have students tap their waist and shoulders to match the two pitches that the saxophone plays. Repeat several times and see how well they are doing!

Tip from Kim

Encourage children to seek out different partners each time because they never know when they'll find a great musician who is on their musical wave length. Jazz musicians listen closely to each other, work together, and look for opportunities to play or sing with other musicians they have never performed with before. Building community among musicians is essential to jazz groups and trading ideas is a valuable way to grow musically.

Activity 4 / Scat and Answer with Two Pitches

CD-2

Track 5

CD2-Track 5

Step 1:

- Skip this step if you are doing this activity directly after Activity 3.
- Students select partners and face each other.
- Play CD2-Track 5 and direct students to echo sing and perform waist or shoulder tapping that corresponds to the root or 3rd.

Step 2:

- Play CD2-Track 5 again and have students *improvise* their response in the measure after the singer, rather than echoing. They should improvise using only the two pitches they have been practicing, root and 3rd.
- As before, they will use the two measures of open rhythm section playing for reflection.
- *Students all improvise at the same time.* It is a good idea to gradually build self-esteem about singing alone and improvising. Allow everyone to sing at the same time as they try out ideas and then ask for individuals to volunteer to sing solos when they are comfortable.

Step 3: Add movement

Play CD2-Track 5 and direct students to improvise using two pitches, but this time add waist and shoulder movements like before (root and 3rd) while they improvise.

Step 4:

- Play CD2-Track 5 and this time students will improvise with movements alone, taking turns with their partner.
- Each person should use the two bars of reflect time to think about their solo or think about what their partner just sang.
- Pause track periodically for partners to talk about each other's improvisation, being careful to pause during the two measures of reflection time.

Step 5:

At the end of the activity say:
"Hold up one finger if you think the feedback of your partner was helpful. Hold up two fingers if it wasn't helpful. Why do you think it was helpful or not?"

Encourage discussion.

Tip from Margaret & Kim

Expect kids to reflect and be able to discuss what they have heard with more than "it was good." Guide students to discuss why improvisations are good, or why they need improvement. When children can begin to verbalize about improvisation at this level you can expect them to think at a high level as they improvise. Building jazz vocabulary includes being able to describe in detail what you hear in your own, and other's, improvisations. The teacher's role is that of a coach, carefully guiding children by asking questions designed to elicit answers that require inner reflection about sound, phrasing, and style. Refer to the Introduction for a list of questions that are appropriate for these types of reflection activities.

♪ Concert Time

*"You're swinging, you're scatting on two notes, and you understand what you're doing when you scat–you're so wise that it's time to learn a new song called **Impro-Wise!**"*

Activity 5 / *Impro-Wise*

CD-2

Tracks 6–9

CD2-Track 6: *Impro-Wise* **Performance Model, Entire Form, with call-and-response**

CD2-Track 7: *Impro-Wise***, Backing Track, Entire Form, with open improvisation**

CD2-Track 8: *Impro-Wise***, Call-and-Response Section (measures 17–24)**

CD2-Track 9: *Impro-Wise***, Backing Track for Call-and-Response Section (measures 17–24)**

The complete Teacher's Score for Impro-Wise *follows these instructions. Teach all parts by rote.*

Step 1: *Teach melody*

- Begin Chop-Monster Groove, and teach *Impro-Wise* melody (measures 5–16) by breaking parts down into 2- or 4-bar phrases and have students echo your singing. Note that the melody is made up of more than two notes. Students will improvise later in the piece with just two notes over a G chord in the solo section, measures 17–24.
- Play the written piano accompaniment and have students sing the entire melody, or use CD2-Track 6 (or backing track CD2-Track 7).
- Select one student to play the ride cymbal part.

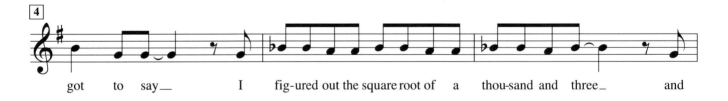

Call-and-Response (repeats measures 17–24)

Step 2: *Call-and-response with two notes (G and B)*
- Divide class into two groups, and form into two lines (longways set).
- Use CD2-Track 8 to practice the call-and-response on two notes.
- Group One will echo sing the *Impro-Wise* phrases while Group Two does waist/shoulder movements to match the pitches. Then Group Two will echo sing the phrases while Group One does waist/shoulder movements.

Step 3:
- Repeat CD2-Track 8 and have all students echo sing and do waist/shoulders movements at the same time. Listen to how well students are matching the pitches that they are singing with their movements.
- Repeat as needed.

Step 4: *Teach Orff parts for solo section (measures 17–24)*
- Begin with ride cymbal and teach Orff parts by rote.
- Bass xylophone plays a steady beat pattern: G for two quarter notes and D for two quarter notes. Or, two students play G and D Bass Boomwhackers with Octivator Caps.
- Alto glockenspiel plays a repeated pattern with two half notes and one whole note, using notes E and A.
- You can add the piano part, but it is optional.

Step 5: *Putting It All Together*
- Play CD2-Track 6 to model song in its entirety, including the introduction and the ending.
- Play backing track CD2-Track 7 and have students sing the melody, play ride cymbal and Orff parts and scat sing during the solo section.
- Or, perform without the recorded accompaniment and play the piano accompaniment while students sing, play ride cymbal and Orff parts.

Impro-Wise

Activity 6 / Improvising on *Impro-Wise*

CD-2
Track 8
Impro-Wise,
Call-and-Response (measures 17–24)

CD-2
Track 9
Impro-Wise,
Backing Track (measures 17–24)

Step 1: Improvise responses

- Review Activity 4 if needed.
- Group One and Group Two form two lines (longways set). Students become partners with the person directly opposite them.
- Be sure to clearly identify which side is Group One because as they work in their partner groups, they will need to know.
- Have partners move closer together so they can hear each other.
- Using CD2-Track 8, Group One people will sing along with the *Impro-Wise* "call" phrases and Group Two people will *improvise* a 2-bar scat response/answer.
- Repeat until Group Two students are answering with ease.

Step 2: Switch Groups

Switch parts so Group Two sings the "call" melodies and Group One improvises 2-bar responses.

Step 3: Try It On Your Own

- Use backing track CD2-Track 9.
- Group One people "call" the *Impro-Wise* phrases *on their own.*
- Group Two people improvise 2-bar scat answers.
- Switch and repeat as needed.
- Optional: Repeat with recorders.

Activity 7 / Got Chops?

This is a reflective activity to encourage higher-level thinking.

Worksheet 9: Got Chops?

Step 1:

- Ask students to sit down next to their partners.
- Pass out photocopies of Worksheet 9: Got Chops?
- Students should answer worksheet questions for themselves and for their partner.
- Partners go over their worksheets with each other.

Step 2:

- Read through each question asking for Group One people to give some answers and Group Two people to give answers.
- Summarize this reflection activity by repeating some of the good answers, reminding students that sharing thoughts and ideas is how jazz musicians express themselves musically, and that you appreciate the good spirit they have used in sharing reflections with each other. It's a big step toward being a Chop-Monster.

<table>
<tr><td colspan="3">Worksheet 9: Got Chops? Thinking About Improvisation
Full Name _____</td></tr>
<tr><td></td><td>Partner 1</td><td>Partner 2</td></tr>
<tr><td>Were the solos interesting to listen to? Why or why not?</td><td></td><td></td></tr>
<tr><td>Did the solos have a feeling that was expressed to the listeners?</td><td></td><td></td></tr>
<tr><td>What ideas did you hear in your partner's solos that you might use in your future solos?</td><td></td><td></td></tr>
</table>

150 | *Chop-Monster Jr.*

⊙ Sitting In

The following activities reference resources that are not included with *Chop-Monster Jr.*, such as audio and video recordings and children's literature. We offer these lesson-enrichment ideas to help increase student awareness about the lives and contributions of the great jazz masters.

Link to Jazz Masters: Riffing with Count Basie

William "Count" Basie (1904–1984)

*"One of the greatest jazz big bands was led by pianist Count Basie. He was born in 1904. He played in a number of big bands in Kansas City, Missouri in the late 1920s and eventually formed his own jazz orchestra. They had a different sound compared to big bands from New York, such as the Duke Ellington Orchestra. Count Basie's band played music that was often made up on the spot by people playing in different sections (saxophones, trombones, trumpets or rhythm). For example, the rhythm section might begin with a jazz groove; someone in the trumpet section might improvise a short idea and quietly play it to the other trumpets and then they start to play that idea louder with the rhythm section. The trumpets might play it in **harmony**, with two or more nice-sounding notes at a time. So now there might be the rhythm section playing, and trumpets, and all of a sudden a tenor saxophone player might think of a good thing to play that responds to the trumpet idea. The saxophone player plays that idea to the other saxophones and they all join in.*

Count Basie

Courtesy of the Institute of Jazz Studies

*"When musicians repeat a catchy musical idea or phrase, it is called a **riff**. Lots of the greatest songs that the early Count Basie Orchestra played were based on riffs. When a soloist is improvising, a section might also begin to play a riff to help the solo build in excitement. Sometimes a section might begin a riff at the end of a solo to imply, 'Hey, here we are, it's time to let someone else solo!' "*

Besides Count Basie on piano, some of the great players who played in the early Count Basie band were Lester Young and Ben Webster on tenor saxophone, Buck Clayton and Harry 'Sweets' Edison on trumpet, and Dicky Wells and Al Grey on trombones. Walter Page played bass and Jo Jones played drums.

Riffing with Count Basie

Listening: Jumpin' at the Woodside

Locate a recording of The Count Basie Orchestra performing "Jumpin' at the Woodside" on _Best of Early Basie_ (Verve). Also available on Disc 2, _Ken Burns Jazz: The Story of America's Music_ 5-CD set (Sony).

Discussion points after repeated listening:

What gives the arrangement its "jumping" sound?

(The Count Basie Orchestra included a guitarist named Freddie Green, whose swinging accompaniment gave the band a distinctive and driving sound. Point out the drummer's ride-cymbal pattern and the bass player's steady beat.)

Discuss the Count Basie Orchestra's use of riffs, both as melodic devices, and behind soloists.

Encourage your students to sing or hum the background riffs along with the recording.

Repeat recording several times so students begin to hum sections of the solos, or recognize when the soloist has changed.

The soloists can be easily heard because the rest of the band is sensitive to the fact that they are in the spotlight. Engage students in discussion about how each soloist has a highly individualized style and ask guiding questions about the feelings each musician might have been trying to communicate.

Note that the soloists begin to trade ideas and overlap their solos toward the end, which makes the arrangement very exciting!

Link to Literature

Who Bop?

Read aloud _Who Bop?_ by Jonathon London and illustrated by Henry Cole (HarperCollins Publishers). Hip hares and cool cats dance to the swinging music of Jazz-bo's saxophone. Practice reading the book with a swing feel before you read it to the children.

Optional: Read along to a recording of "Lester Leaps In" included on Ken Burns _Jazz: The Story of America's Music,_ Disc 3.

Link to History

Jazz: A Film by Ken Burns

Episode 6, _Jazz: A Film by Ken Burns_ (PBS Home Video), DVD or videocassettes. www.pbs.org/jazz

Jazz for Young People Curriculum

Lesson 7, _Jazz for Young People Curriculum_, Marsalis, New York: Jazz at Lincoln Center, 2002, compact discs/teacher's guide/student guides. www.jazzatlincolncenter.org

Websites:

Ken Burns Jazz

Photographs, sound clips and more of the Count Basie Orchestra. www.pbs.org/jazz/biography/artist_id_basie_count.htm

A Great Day in Harlem

Great information on Count Basie and his band. http://www.harlem.org/people/basie.html

Cooking in Jazz

- Creating a rhythm section
- Independent music makers
- Improvising on two pitches (C & E)

Preparing for Success

✅ Jam Session

Students will assume roles of the rhythm section by independently playing parts on classroom instruments that correspond with jazz piano, bass and drumset. Students will create their own arrangement, and improvise with two pitches.

Activity 1: Listen to the Rhythm Section
Activity 2: Sticky Situation Rhythm Section
Activity 3: Transferring to Instruments
Activity 4: *Sticky Situation*
Activity 5: Cookin' with the Rhythm Section
Activity 6: Creating an Arrangement
Activity 7: Comparing Class Recording to CD
Link: Dizzy Gillespie and Charlie Parker

Vocabulary

Rhythm section, walking bass, hi-hat, ride cymbal, arrangement, improviser, solo

Materials

- *Chop-Monster Jr.* CD2-Tracks 10–19
- Worksheet 10: Cookin' with the Rhythm Section
- Worksheet 11: Jammin' on Sticky Situation
- Worksheet 12: Two Versions of Sticky Situation
- Worksheet 13: "Salt Peanuts" Listening Map
- Ride cymbal and drumstick
- Alto and soprano glockenspiels with 2 mallets (E and A)
- Alto and soprano xylophones with 2 mallets (C)
- Bass xylophone with 2 mallets (C, A, G, E) or, C, A, G and E Bass Boomwhackers
- Soprano recorders, optional (two notes: C and E)

Indicators of Success

Students will play parts that correspond with jazz piano, bass and drumset parts. Students improvise their own jazz melodies using two notes. Students successfully create a new arrangement of *Sticky Situation*.

♪ Concert Time

Students will demonstrate their understanding of the roles of jazz rhythm section players through independent performance of *Sticky Situation*. Students will improvise on two pitches during their performance.

💿 Sitting In

Students will learn through suggested learning links about Dizzy Gillespie and Charlie Parker and their contribution to the jazz world: bebop!

Unless specified, you will need to supply the referenced audio or video recordings.

Link to Jazz Masters

"Salt Peanuts," John Gillespie. *Ken Burns Jazz: The Story of America's Music,* Disc 3, Columbia/Legacy 5-CD set (from *Shaw Nuff*, Musicraft/Discovery), audio recording. www.legacyrecordings.com

"Salt Peanuts," is also available on Dizzy Gillespie and His All Star Quintet, *Definitive Dizzy Gillespie*, Verve, audio recording. www.vervemusicgroup.com

"Night in Tunisia," John Gillespie, Frank Paparelli. Charlie Parker and Dizzy Gillespie from *Complete Savoy Masters, Charlie Parker*, Definitive Records, audio recording.

"Now's the Time," Charles Parker Jr. *The Quartet of Charlie Parker.* Verve, audio recording. www.vervemusicgroup.com

Link to Literature

Charlie Parker played be bop, Chris Raschka. New York: Orchard Books, 1992.

Link to History

Jazz: A Film by Ken Burns, Episode 8, Florentine Films/PBS/Warner Home Video, video recording (also DVD). www.pbs.org/jazz

Jazz for Young People Curriculum, Lesson 12, Marsalis, New York: Jazz at Lincoln Center, 2002, teaching curriculum with 30 student guides. 10-CD set audio recordings and video recording. www.jazzatlincolncenter.org

✔ Jam Session

Introduction

*"We have learned that when a soloist improvises, they express themselves through their solos. We have been singing, moving and playing instruments to a jazz group on the CD. The type of jazz group you have been hearing is a **rhythm section**. A jazz rhythm section is usually made up of a piano, bass and drumset. There may be a guitar or vibes, too.*

"The rhythm section is really important because it establishes the tempo, groove, dynamics, and harmony. If other jazz instrumentalists such as saxophone, trumpet or trombone are also performing, they listen carefully to the rhythm section, and vice versa, and the end result is exciting because the music is created "in the moment." The rhythm section can play rhythms or accompaniments that inspire improvisers to come up with new ideas or go in interesting directions with their solos. We are going to learn to perform like a rhythm section. Later, we will take turns improvising to our rhythm section creations."

Activity 1 / Listen to the Rhythm Section

CD-2
 Track 10

Jazz Rhythm Section

Reproducible Worksheet 1: Jazz Instruments

"On this recording you will hear a rhythm section with three instruments playing. As you listen, do the Chop-Monster Groove and see if you can identify the three instruments on the recording."

Step 1:

Play CD2-Track 10 and model the Chop-Monster Groove as students listen. Students should quickly be able to do the groove.

Step 2:

- *"Who can name an instrument they heard in the recording?"*
- As students name the instruments they hear, reinforce correct answers: piano, bass, or drums.
- If you wish, use Worksheet 1: Jazz Instruments to show illustrations of the instruments.

Step 3:

Play CD2-Tracks 11, 12 and 13 that demonstrate each rhythm section instrument separately, and introduce each instrument as follows. The first instrument is the upright string bass:

Bass

CD-2
 Track 11

Jazz Bass

*"The bass in a jazz rhythm section will play what jazz musicians call a **walking bass** line. Let's listen to how the bass sounds alone."*

Play bass-only CD2-Track 11 and discuss.

Step 4:

"Let's listen again and imitate the walking bass line by patting our legs while we say "Chew-ing, chew-ing.""

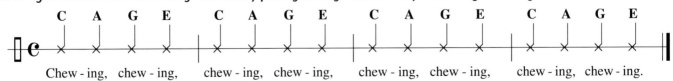

Play CD2-Track 11 again, model leg pats for walking bass line, and practice with entire class.

Step 5:
Piano

CD-2

Track 12 **Jazz Piano**

"Let's listen to how the piano is often played in a rhythm section."

> Play piano-only CD2-Track 12 and discuss.

"Let's imitate the piano part by clapping and chanting 'yum-my, gum-my!'"

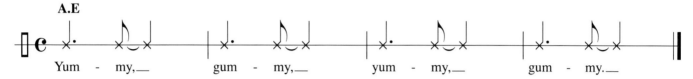

Step 6:
- Practice clapping and chanting to CD2-Track 12 with entire class.
- Combine the bass and piano body percussion parts you practiced by splitting class into two parts and get the first part going and then bring the second one in.
  - Part 1 is the walking bass line (Chew-ing, Chew-ing…)
  - Part 2 is the piano (yum-my gum-my…)

Step 7:
Drumset

CD-2

Track 13 **Jazz Drums**

"Listen for different parts of the drumset on the recording. Who can name some parts of the drumset?"

> Play drumset-only CD2-Track 13 and reinforce correct answers: hi-hat,
> ride cymbal, drums.

Step 8:

"Let's create the sound of the hi-hat. A hi-hat is two cymbals that close together when the drummer presses and releases a foot pedal. The hi-hat plays the groove on beats 2 & 4 that you all do so well."

> Play CD2-Track 13 again and have students tap/clap the Chop-Monster Groove as they listen.

"I would like you to snap your fingers to the groove and say, '(rest) snap, (rest) crack, (rest) crunch, (rest) pop!'"

> Practice this part with the entire class.

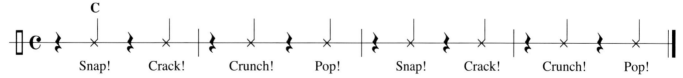

Step 9:
- Break class into Parts 1, 2 and 3 and combine all three parts together, starting one part at a time and layering them in.
- Repeat until the groove "clicks." If needed, chant "doodle-dah" or "doo-dah" quietly to help students feel the triplet and swing eighth note subdivision.
  - Part 1 is the walking bass line (Chew-ing, Chew-ing…)
  - Part 2 is the piano (yum-my gum-my…)
  - Part 3 is the hi-hat (snap, crack, crunch, pop…)

Step 10:

"The last part of the drumset is the ride cymbal which we have played several times in class. Let's listen to the drummer's ride cymbal and chant our 'gum, bubble gum' rhythm. Rub your hands together to the rhythm."

Play CD2: Track 13 and practice until comfortable for class. This rhythm was introduced in Unit 1/Part 1/Activity 6, *Jazzy Ride*.

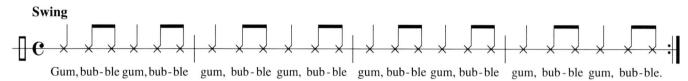

Activity 2 / Sticky Situation Rhythm Section

"Now we are going to put the rhythm section all together. It's important for each part to chant while doing the body percussion. We're going to call ourselves the Sticky Situation Rhythm Section."

Break class into four sections and have them stand or sit next to each other.
- Part 1 is the walking bass line (Chew-ing, Chew-ing…)
- Part 2 is the piano (yum-my gum-my…)
- Part 3 is the hi-hat (snap, crack, crunch, pop…)
- Part 4 is the ride cymbal (gum, bubble gum…)

Layer in the parts. You can layer out parts to hear different parts and to give students the opportunity to hear different combinations of the parts. Your students should focus on hearing how they fit together and contribute to the groove or swing feel.

Activity 3 / Transferring to Instruments
- Review Activity 1 if you are coming back to this activity on a new day.
- If you do not have instruments, just continue with body percussion.
- If using Orff instruments, you will need one each of the following:
  - Bass xylophone (C, A, G, E)
  - Alto and soprano xylophones (C)
  - Alto and soprano glockenspiels (A and E)
  - You will also need a ride cymbal and drumstick
- If you do not have a bass xylophone, use bass Boomwhackers using the following notes, played one child per Boomwhacker, or two children with two Boomwhackers each: (C, A, G, E)
- Instructions given here are for Orff instruments; adapt as needed.

Tip From Margaret

As mentioned in Unit 1, I have found that Boomwhackers sound a lot better and louder if you play them on carpeting or carpet squares. I ALWAYS use the octivator caps because it makes them less "thwacky" sounding. When using Boomwhackers for this activity, hold them upright with the octivator cap on the bottom. The octivator cap is the part that hits the rug.

Step 1:

"Let's transfer your body percussion to instruments. Bass people are going to play their part on the bass xylophone. Then you will all take turns trying this."

- If playing bass xylophone, have one student at a time transfer the pattern to C, A, G, E on the bass xylophone.
- Or transfer the pattern to C, A, C, E, with one child per bass Boomwhacker.

Sticky Situation
Rhythm Section

- Students not playing an instrument should continue to do Parts 1, 2, 3 and 4 body percussion (as taught in Activity 1) and chant to help students on bass xylophone play with steady beat.
- If desired, have some students tap/clap the Chop-Monster Groove.
- Have students take turns at the bass xylophone.

Step 2:

"Let's get the hi-hat cymbal people to take their groove and put it on the soprano and alto xylophones."

- Using two mallets each, students play Cs together on their respective instruments on beats 2 & 4.
- Again have students not playing do body percussion and chant part to help others.
- Switch people so everyone gets a chance on the instruments.

Step 3:

"Let's now add the ride cymbal people."

- Show students again how to hold the drum stick and play the ride-cymbal pattern (as introduced in Unit 1/Part 1/Activity 6 *Jazzy Ride*).
- Important: use no more than one ride cymbal so the time stays together.
- Students not playing should do body percussion and chant.
- Switch people around so everyone has a chance to try the cymbal.

Step 4:

"The piano is the last part. I need people to play soprano and alto glockenspiels on A and E."

- Using two mallets each, students play A and E together on their respective instruments using the piano rhythm.
- Have students not playing instruments do body percussion and chant.
- Switch people around so everyone gets to try it.

Step 5:

- Layer in parts beginning with bass, add "hi-hat," then ride cymbal and finally "piano." Layer parts in and out but keep bass always playing. This helps students to hear how the parts fit with each other and promotes them to play with more independence.
- Switch parts so everyone gets a turn to play with the entire rhythm section.
- As students become more secure on their individual parts you can begin to take away body percussion and chanting.

♪ Concert Time

Activity 4: *Sticky Situation*

CD-2
Track 14
Sticky Situation,
Performance Model

CD-2
Track 15
Sticky Situation,
Backing Track (rhythm section background)

Step 1:

"We're going to get our Sticky Situation Rhythm Section groove going again, and learn a melody that goes along with it. Then we will improvise to Sticky Situation."

- Play the first part of CD2-Track 14 to model the melody and rhythm parts.
- Teach the 8-measure melody by echo singing in four bar phrases.
- Layer in the four parts of the *Sticky Situation* rhythm section as you did in Activity 2.
- Play along with CD2-Track 15, which is a backing track without the melody.

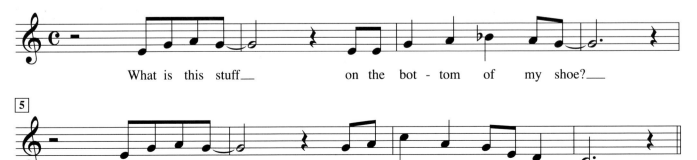

Sticky Situation

Scatch-mo Station Room Setup Diagram

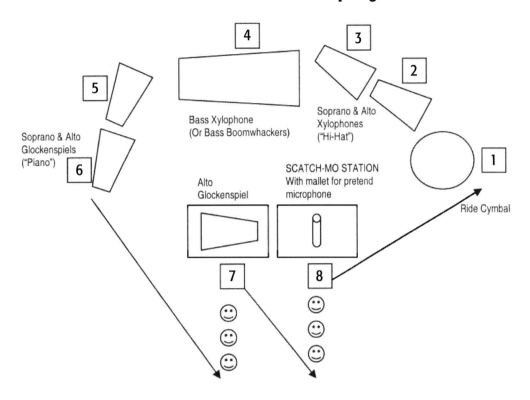

Step 2:

"Now we're going to have some fun taking turns on all of the parts, as well as improvising and scat singing to Sticky Situation. You will use two notes, C and E, for your solos, so it will be easy! We're going to use a room setup called Scatch-mo Station."

- Set up instruments in your classroom to match the Scatch-mo Station room setup diagram, making sure students will have eye contact with each other. You will ask for eight volunteers and assign one person to each per station. Additional students will line up behind Station 7 and Station 8 for their turn to improvise on an instrument and scat sing.

- At one end of the room is the "rhythm section." Make sure children can see each other:
  - Station 1: Ride cymbal
  - Station 2: "Hi-hat" use alto xylophone
  - Station 3: "Hi-hat" use soprano xylophone
  - Station 4: "Bass" use bass xylophone
  - Station 5: "Piano" use soprano glockenspiel
  - Station 6: "Piano" use alto glockenspiel
- The "rhythm section" will face the improvisers who are on the other side of the room in two lines:
- Station 7: One barred instrument set on a table, such as soprano or alto glockenspiel. Improvisers form a line behind this station for their turn to improvise.
- Station 8: "Scatch-mo Station" for scat singers. Provide a prop to use as a pretend microphone, such as an Orff mallet. Scat singers form a line behind this station for their turn to improvise.

Step 3:

"You will cycle through the stations in order: ride cymbal will move to alto xylophone, and then to soprano xylophone to play the 'hi-hat' parts; then to bass xylophone to play the 'bass' part; then to alto glockenspiel and soprano glockenspiel to play the 'piano' parts.

"After that you will leave the rhythm section and go to the end of the instrument improviser's line. When you've moved forward through the instrument improviser's line you will take your turn to play a solo on the glockenspiel for four measures, and then move to the end of the Scatch-mo Station line to wait for your turn to scat.

"When you finish your 4-bar scat solo at the Scatch-mo Station, you move to the ride cymbal. When the person who was first to play the ride cymbal at Station 1 gets back to the ride cymbal, the song will be complete.

"In between each improvised solo, we will chant for four measures to give us time to move to our new positions. We will use a chant we already know: 'Gum, bubble gum.'"

Swing

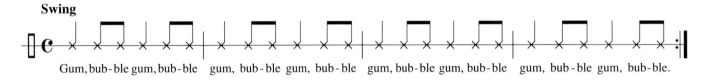

Gum, bub-ble gum, bub-ble   gum, bub-ble gum, bub-ble   gum, bub-ble gum, bub-ble   gum, bub-ble gum, bub-ble.

Optional:

> When rotating from station to station the first few times it may be helpful to chant:
> "ONE bubble gum bubble,
> TWO bubble gum bubble,
> THREE bubble gum bubble,
> FOUR bubble gum bubble."

Step 4: Combining All Parts in the Orff Rhythm Section

CD-2
Track 15
Sticky Situation,
Backing Track

"Now it's time to add all the parts together for a performance!"

- With or without CD2-Track 15, layer in the parts beginning with "bass," "hi-hat," ride cymbal, "piano" and have children who are standing in the two lines behind Station 7 and Station 8 sing the melody.
- Repeat as many times as desired, and end either by layering parts back out, or fading out, or ending on the last note.

Step 5: *Orff Rhythm Section Alone, and add improvisation*

"And now we're going to rotate around the stations and take turns improvising. When you get to the front of the line at Station 7 you will improvise a 4-bar solo on the barred instrument, and then quietly move to the end of the Scatch-mo Station line while the person who is at the front of the Scatch-mo Station line scat sings a 4-bar solo. At that point we will chant 'Gum, bubble gum' for four measures and rotate stations. Remember, you are using only two notes, C and E when you improvise."

- Encourage bass and cymbal parts to respond to each soloist's dynamic level as they play their parts so each soloist can be heard.
- Have students who are standing in line sing the melody at the beginning and at the end of the song.
- While improvisers are playing, those standing in line can do body percussion such as rubbing hands to the ride-cymbal pattern, doing the Chop-Monster Groove, and so on.
- Remember to chant "gum, bubble gum" for four measures as students rotate to different stations.

Step 5: *Try It On Your Own*

CD-2
Track 15

Sticky Situation,
Backing Track

- You do not need to rotate stations for this step.
- With or without backing track CD2-Track 15, perform *Sticky Situation* by layering in rhythm section parts and cue a group of students to sing the melody.
- Repeat the *Sticky Situation* groove over and over to give everyone a chance to sing or play solos if they want.
- Once students are comfortable soloing for four bars, you can have them play and scat 8-bar solos.
- End by cueing a group of students to sing the melody again. You may either hold the last note of the melody for a cut off, or layer parts out for a fade ending.

Tip from Margaret

It is important to maintain a groove while children are soloing. In order to keep the music flowing, I ask that anyone who wants to solo put up one finger indicating that they would like to solo next. Since students need to indicate they want to solo beforehand, it shows that they can "hear" when a solo break is coming—how cool is that? If you are making an audio recording your performance, say each student's name into the recorder before they begin their solo by announcing "It's Pete in, 1-, 2-, 1, 2, 3, 4." That way when you replay the recording for kids to evaluate, they will know who played each solo.

♪ Concert Time

Sing melody first time.

On repeats, Station 7 student improvises a solo on a barred instrument for measures 1–4;

then Station 8 (Scatch-Mo Station) student improvises a scat vocal solo for measures 5–8.

Students chant "gum, bubble gum, bubble" for 4 measures (measures 9–12) while rotating stations.

Repeat as desired for improvisation.

Sing melody last time and hold "C" at measure 8.

Sticky Situation

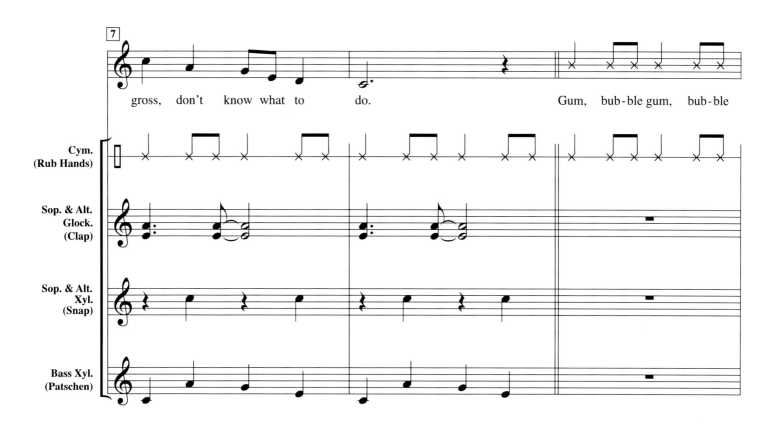

gross, don't know what to do.   Gum, bub-ble gum, bub-ble

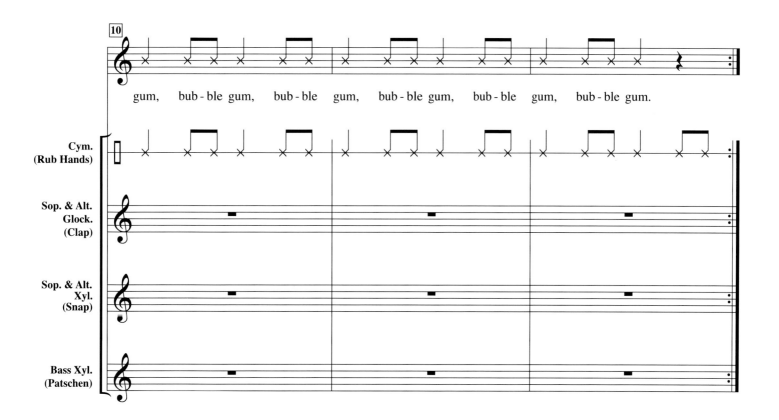

gum, bub-ble gum, bub-ble gum, bub-ble gum, bub-ble gum, bub-ble gum.

Activity 5 / Cookin' with the Rhythm Section

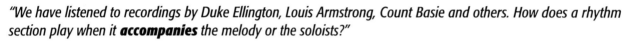

Worksheet 10: Cookin' with the Rhythm Section

If you don't plan to collect and grade worksheets, be sure you tell the students that. We recommend that you do not grade this activity; just explain that it's for listening with better ears. If you do want to collect them for grading, then collect them before going over what is on the worksheets but write students' answers on the board.

Step 1:

"Let's think back to when we played Sticky Situation *and we all played our solos with the rhythm section. What did we have to do to make it work?"*

> Answers should include balance, hear the solo, play or sing with emotion.

*"We have listened to recordings by Duke Ellington, Louis Armstrong, Count Basie and others. How does a rhythm section play when it **accompanies** the melody or the soloists?"*

> Write answers on the board. Tell students they can add answers from the board to their worksheets to help them remember to use some of the techniques in their solos.

Step 2: Listen and Fill In Worksheet 10

Cookin' Rhythm Section, with Soloist
(same as Jazzy Sax Plays Two Pitches)

"Let's listen to the jazz group on the CD playing together. We are going to hear the rhythm section playing with an improvised solo. I would like you to listen and see if you can tell whether the rhythm section does a good job of backing the soloist. Remember the soloist is the most important thing and the rhythm section works in the background to help the soloist cook up a really tasty soup—the soloist floats on top of all the good stuff below."

> Play CD2-Track 4 and have children write some observations in "Good" or "Not So Good" box next to Recording #1 heading on Worksheet 10, focusing on how well the rhythm section accompanies the soloist. Discuss and compare to answers written on board.

Step 3:

"Inappropriate" Rhythm Section, with Soloist

> Play CD2-Track 16 (it is similar to Track 4 but there are some glaring balance problems in rhythm section such as):
> - Drummer: bass drum and snare drum are too loud
> - Bass: playing staccato instead of legato
> - Piano: holding damper pedal down too long and playing too many accompaniment rhythms
>
> Have children write some observations about this out-of-balance recording, next to Recording #2 heading on Worksheet 10. Discuss and compare to answers written on board.

Step 4:

Cookin' Orff Rhythm Section, with Scat Singer

"Let's listen to an Orff rhythm section and see how well they do with a scat singer."

> Play CD2-Track 17 and have students write observations on their worksheets, next to Recording #3 heading on Worksheet 10. Summarize on the board.

Step 5:

CD-2
Track 18

"Inappropriate" Orff Rhythm Section, with Scat Singer

"Let's listen to a different Orff rhythm section and compare."

Play CD2-Track 18 and have students write observations on their worksheets, next to Recording #4 heading on Worksheet 10. Summarize on the board again. Examples of inappropriate accompanying are:

- Ride cymbal—too loud
- Bass xylophone or Boomwhackers—unsteady beat

Step 6: *Optional*

Compare to a recording of your class. Have students write observations on their worksheets, next to Recording #5 heading on Worksheet 10.

Activity 6 / Creating an Arrangement of *Sticky Situation*

Step 1:

Remind students that famous jazz groups like the Count Basie Band made up arrangements on the spot by layering in background riffs and harmony, melody and solos. Once again, take the role of a coach and have your class decide on an arrangement of *Sticky Situation*. The arrangement can include layering of parts, having parts play alone or in combinations, using body percussion, using chanting, solos, the melody and movement. There are many ways the song can be developed; try out different ideas.

Step 2:

Make sure to use ideas from all the children who volunteer them. Perform them and then ask each child if they liked the way their idea sounded. Why or why not? This helps children to become independent music makers.

Step 3:

Worksheet 11: Jammin' on *Sticky Situation*
Come up with a final arrangement and have the group perform it. Record it and have the class answer questions using Worksheet 11: Jammin' on *Sticky Situation*.

Step 4:

Play recording and ask students to answer questions on the worksheet. Feel free to stop the recording at any time to focus on something that needs it. Listening to the entire tune is great, but it is useful and illuminating to listen and critique little bits, like a solo or two and then put the whole together. The point is to reflect on the solos and discuss how they sound, how the performer developed their chops.

Step 5:

Discuss answers with class and be sure to give children lots of opportunities to think about and talk about the arrangement and performance of *Sticky Situation*.

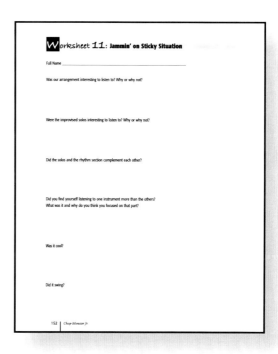

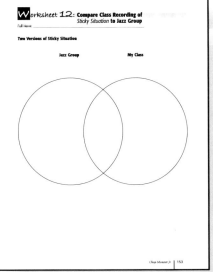

Activity 7 / Comparing Class Recording of *Sticky Situation* to Jazz Group on the CD

Worksheet 12: Two Versions of *Sticky Situation*

Step 1:

"You are going to hear a new version of Sticky Situation *by the jazz group on the CD. The arrangement and the sound will be different than our class recording, but both versions are jazz—they both include improvisation and of course great swing feel. We're going to identify what are the* same *and* different *about the two versions."*

Pass out and explain Worksheet 12: Two Versions of *Sticky Situation*:

- There are two circles that overlap. In the middle section, where the circles overlap, students should write down things that are the same about the class version of *Sticky Situation* and the CD jazz group's performance of *Sticky Situation* (examples: swing feel, improvisation, walking bass line).
- In the left circle, students fill in things they hear in the jazz group's version that are *different* from their version: (more elaborate piano rhythms that change as the song goes on, drum kicks and fills, dynamics, building excitement, walking bass line may have different notes).

Step 2:

CD-2
Track 19

Jazz Group's version of *Sticky Situation*

Play CD2-Track 19, jazz group's version of *Sticky Situation*.
"What are some of the things you heard that are different?*"*

Use guiding questions suggested in Introduction to get students to think deeply about what they heard. Have them write down their observations in the left circle of the worksheet.

Step 3:

Class recording of *Sticky Situation*

"Now listen to the recording of our class performing Sticky Situation. *List things that are* different *about our performance in the right circle. Write down anything else that is the same in the section where the circles overlap."*

Students should have a few new observations about the class version after listening to and talking about the jazz group version. They will have new concepts that emerge from hearing the jazz group version. The more noticeable things that students should be able to identify are the elaboration of the rhythm section parts— the arrangement that your students created will most likely have stayed pretty constant where the rhythm section parts don't change much.

Step 4:

Ask students to share their answers again. Discuss how they might integrate some of the things they noticed in the jazz group's version into their class version.

Tip from Kim

As students share their observations, write some of the ideas on a large Venn diagram (overlapped circles), either on the board or on a big sheet of paper for the whole group to see. Your students are developing words for abstract thoughts and sounds and may need you to help them with correct music terminology to describe what they heard (decrescendo, etc.) This is a very valuable piece toward getting children to move through higher and more complex layers of musical creation. If you have time in your curriculum, try out some of their observations and ideas after they have heard the jazz group's version. This is a very rich experience in thinking about music that will come through in so many things they experience in your music classes. Nurture this!

⇨ Sitting In

The following activities reference resources that are not included with *Chop-Monster Jr.,* such as audio and video recordings and children's literature. We offer these lesson-enrichment ideas to help increase student awareness about the lives and contributions of the great jazz masters.

*"The rhythm section is an important component of any jazz group. You have listened to some examples of swinging rhythm sections in The Duke Ellington Orchestra and The Count Basie Orchestra. In the 1940s, a new style of jazz emerged called **bebop**. The bands were smaller, the music was fast, unpredictable and exciting, and it showcased incredible soloists! The music was still swinging, but it was not for dancing. Two musicians in particular led the way and showed others how to play bebop. They were Dizzy Gillespie and Charlie Parker. Dizzy played the trumpet and Charlie played the alto saxophone.*

"We'll first learn about Dizzy Gillespie, and listen to the way his bebop rhythm section accompanied the bebop soloists, and then we'll learn about Charlie Parker."

Dizzy Gillespie

Link to Jazz Masters: Innovating with Dizzy Gillespie

John "Dizzy" Gillespie (1917–1993)

"Dizzy Gillespie's first name was John, but everyone called him Dizzy. He had a great sense of humor and was always playing tricks on people and having lots of fun. He even got fired from a job for throwing spitballs during a performance. Dizzy had a trumpet that was accidentally knocked over and bent so the trumpet bell pointed upwards. Dizzy thought it sounded even better bent that way so he kept it like that.

"Dizzy was also a trend setter. People all over the world copied the way he dressed and looked. For a while, people wore a goatee like Dizzy, or a beret (a flat little hat) like Dizzy.

"So now you can probably figure out why they called him Dizzy: he was often doing something crazy and wild and his trumpet playing could also be very crazy and wild. We're going to listen to a recording of Dizzy's called 'Salt Peanuts,' but before I play it can someone tell what they think we might hear in this recording? What do you think Dizzy might sound like? Let's see if you are right."

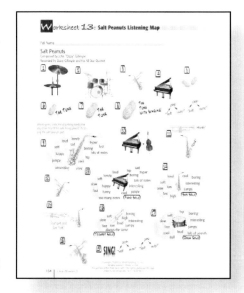

Teacher's Guide to Listening Activity

Innovating with Dizzy Gillespie

Worksheet 13: Salt Peanuts Listening Map

Listening: Salt Peanuts

Locate a recording of "Salt Peanuts" by Dizzy Gillespie, *Definitive Dizzy Gillespie* (Verve) or *Ken Burns Jazz: The Story of America's Music* (Sony). There are numbers printed on the listening map that correspond directly to the form of the piece. Please listen to the recording before doing this activity so you are comfortable calling out the numbers for your students.

"You will be listening to a recording of a piece composed and performed by Dizzy Gillespie. It is called 'Salt Peanuts.' As you listen, you'll be following a listening map. You'll need to follow the numbers that are called out in order to keep your place on the listening map. The larger 'peanuts' with words in them are for you! Circle the words that best describe the solo you are listening to at that time."

- Distribute Listening Map for "Salt Peanuts" and pencils.
- Make sure everyone understands what the map symbols mean (trumpet, sax, piano, drumset, cymbal, walking bass).
- Fast forward the recording to a place with obvious walking bass—like in the piano solo (numbered 13 on listening map). Have students listen and express why it is called "walking" bass." Walk two fingers on your opposite palm or up your opposite arm and back down and ask guiding question such as, "How does the bass sound? Why do you suppose it's called a 'walking' bass? Is it a steady beat?"
- Play the recording twice while students follow along on the listening map. They will circle the descriptive words on the first listening. The second listening will allow students to listen and follow the map without circling words.
- Ask for volunteers to tell the class which word(s) they circled for each solo and why. In order to do this, play the recording, follow map, listen to solo at No. 9 on the listening map, pause CD and discuss,
  release pause and listen, pause at No. 13 on the listening map, and so on.
  Optional: listen once again all the way through, and this time, have the class sing along whenever the "salt peanuts" tune comes along!

Bonus question:

"Who do you think was playing the saxophone on that recording?"

Students should remember that Charlie Parker played with Dizzy.

Link to Jazz Masters: Now's the Time for Charlie Parker

Charlie Parker (1920–1955)

"Charlie Parker was from Kansas City, Missouri. Born in 1920, he was one of the greatest saxophone players in jazz. He played alto saxophone. His nickname was Bird, or Yardbird. Some say it was because he liked chicken. Others say it was because as a teenager he used to get up early before school and go to the park to play jazz with his friends—it was Charlie getting up early and singing with the birds. Charlie Parker's impact on jazz was so immediate that he was a legend in his own lifetime, even though he only lived until the age of 35."

Photo: © Robert Parent

Charlie Parker

Teacher's Guide to Listening Activity

Now's the Time for Charlie Parker

Listening: Night in Tunisia
Locate and play a recording of "Night in Tunisia" by Dizzy Gillespie, recorded by Charlie Parker and Dizzy Gillespie on *Complete Savoy Masters*, (Definitive Records DRCD11140).

Link to Literature

Charlie Parker played be bop
Read aloud *Charlie Parker played be bop* by Chris Raschka (Orchard Books). Take your time reading the book. Explain to students that the text of the book was written to loosely work with the melody of "Night in Tunisia" composed by Dizzy Gillespie.
Optional: Read along to "Night in Tunisia" from Charlie Parker Coplete Savoy Masters (DRCD11140) or a recording of "Ko-Ko" on Ken Burns *Jazz: The Story of America's Music,* Disc 3.

Listening: Now's the Time

Locate and play a recording of "Now's the Time" by Charlie Parker, *The Quartet of Charlie Parker* (Verve).

"Does Charlie Parker sound the way you thought he would from the story book? How would you describe Charlie Parker's improvisations compared to everything we have listened to so far?"

Link to History

Jazz: A Film by Ken Burns

Episodes 7 and 8 of *Jazz: A Film by Ken Burns* focus on bebop, Dizzy Gillespie and Charlie Parker (PBS Home Video, DVD/videocassette).
www.pbs.org/jazz

Jazz for Young People Curriculum

Lesson 12 highlights Charlie Parker and Lesson 13 highlights Dizzy Gillespie in the *Jazz for Young People Curriculum*, Marsalis, New York: Jazz at Lincoln Center, 2002, compact discs/teacher's guide/student guides.
www.jazzatlincolncenter.org

Websites:

Ken Burns Jazz Kids

The "Now and Then" portion of Ken Burns Jazz Kids website features a biography of Charlie Parker.
http://www.pbs.org/jazz/kids/nowthen/parker.html

Ken Burns Jazz Website

Biographies of both Dizzy Gillespie and Charlie Parker are featured on this website, plus audio examples.
http://www.pbs.org/jazz/biography/artist_id_parker_charlie.htm

Jamming in Jazz

- Scat singing on three pitches
- Improvisation on three pitches (F, A, C)

Preparing for Success

✓ Jam Session

Students will reflect on the ways the rhythm section works well with the melody and soloists and apply techniques to their own playing.

Students will echo sing and scat sing solos on three pitches using swing feel. Students will do corresponding movements to improvisation.

> Activity 1: Hip Scat and Groove on Three Pitches
> Activity 2: Hip Scat and Move on Three Pitches
> Activity 3: Improvising on Three Pitches
> Activity 4: Scattin' with the Rhythm Section
> Activity 5: *Feelin' Mighty Hip*
> Activity 6: Jammin' on *Feeling Mighty Hip*
> Link: Miles Davis

Vocabulary

Hip, cat, accompany, comp, trade fours

Materials

- *Chop-Monster Jr.* CD2-Tracks 20–25
- Ride cymbal with drumstick
- Soprano and alto glockenspiels with 2 mallets (D, E, A)
- Soprano and alto xylophones with 2 mallets (F)
- Bass xylophone with mallets (F, D, C, A) or, F, D, C, A Bass Boomwhackers

Indicators of Success

Students reflected on the ways the rhythm section works well with the melody and soloists and apply techniques to their own playing.

Students scat sung on three pitches using swing feel. Students performed improvised movements and played instruments using three movements/pitches.

♪ Concert Time

Students perform the song *Feelin' Mighty Hip* and improvise with three pitches by scat singing and playing barred instruments.

⊙ Sitting In

Students will learn about the legendary jazz innovator Miles Davis and the cool jazz style through suggested learning links.

Unless specified, you will need to supply the referenced audio or video recordings.

Link to Jazz Masters

"Summertime," George Gershwin, Ira Gershwin. *Porgy and Bess*, Miles Davis. Legacy/Sony, audio recording. www.legacy recordings.com

"Summertime," George Gershwin, Ira Gershwin. *Chop-Monster Jr.* CD2-Track 25. www.alfred.com

Link to Literature

Hip Cat, Jonathan London, illustrated by Woodleigh Hubbard, San Francisco: Chronicle Books, 1993.

Hip Cat Video, narrated by Ann Duquesnay, Reading Rainbow, 1997. GPN Program number 126.127, video recording. http://gpn.unl.edu/rainbow

Lookin' for Bird in the Big City, Robert Burleigh, illustrated by Marek Los. San Diego: Silver Whistle Harcourt, Inc., 2001. www.harcourtbooks.com

Link to History

"All Blues," "So What" and other Miles Davis favorites, are featured in *Jazz: A Film by Ken Burns,* Episode 9, Florentine Films/PBS/Warner Home Video, 10-episode video series (also DVD). www.pbs.org/jazz

Jazz for Young People Curriculum, Lesson 15, Marsalis, 2002, Jazz at Lincoln Center, teaching curriculum with 30 student guides, 10 CD set audio recordings and video recording. www.jazzatlincolncenter.org

✓ Jam Session

Introduction

*"We have learned how to be members of a rhythm section, and we have improvised to our own rhythm section. We also discussed how the rhythm section listens closely to the soloists and **complements** what they play. Let's think about that as we listen and work on our scat singing and instrument improvisations."*

Activity 1: Hip Scat and Groove on Three Pitches

CD-2

 Track 20

Hip Scat and Groove on Three Pitches
(call and response with 2 bars of reflection time)

Step 1:

> Listen to CD2-Track 20 and ask students to only tap/clap the Chop-Monster Groove as they listen completely through the track the first time.

Step 2:

*"Did you notice that the scat singer was improvising using three pitches? Using more notes opens up many interesting possibilities for our solos. When jazz musicians hear a solo that they really like, they say it is **hip**. Let's do some hip scat singing!"*

> Play CD2-Track 20 again and this time direct students to echo sing. They should focus on imitating the singer exactly, matching scat syllables, inflection, phrasing, dynamics, scoops and so on.

Step 3:

- Play CD2-Track 20 again and direct students to do the Chop-Monster Groove as they echo sing. By now they should be imitating the singer pretty well.
- Continue to repeat the track until students are beginning to memorize the jazz phrases.
- Remind students to reflect on their scat singing during the two "open" bars after they sing.

Activity 2 / Hip Scat and Move on Three Pitches

Step 1:

CD-2

 Track 20

Hip Scat and Move on Three Pitches
(call-and-response, no reflection 2-bars)
Using CD2-Track 21, direct students to keep the groove and echo sing. (This time the track does NOT include two bars of open time for reflection.)

Step 2: add movement

- Students select partners and face each other.
- Teach "Chop-Monster Moves" body movements to correspond to three pitches (F, A and C). Lead students in a "Simon says" type of activity and have them sing and show the pitches as follows:
  - F by tapping waist
  - A by tapping shoulders
  - C by tapping head.
- Tell students you will be referring to this type of movement as "Chop-Monster Moves."

Step 3:

- Using CD2-Track 21 again, direct students to echo sing again and add Chop-Monster Moves that correspond to the pitches they are echo-singing.
- Repeat to allow students to practice this activity as many times as you think is necessary so students are able to master singing with the movements.

Activity 3: Hip Improvising on Three Pitches

CD2-Track 21

(again)

Step 1:

- Play CD2-Track 21 again, but this time students improvise using three pitches to the singer's call on the recording. Have students improvise by humming first to build confidence.
- Everyone in the class is improvising at the same time, but students should be looking only at their partner.

Step 2:

Repeat Step 1 with CD2-Track 21 as many times you feel is necessary. Encourage students to do Chop-Monster Moves as they scat.

Step 3:

Using CD2-Track 21, students take turns with partner improvising after the singer's call on the recording.
Repeat and periodically pause recording to ask students to give their partner reflections on their improvisations. Give them a couple of minutes then take the recording off pause and let them continue for awhile and pause again having partners repeat same process.

Step 4:

Play recording to end and let partners give feedback to each other one more time. Then say:
 "Hold up one finger if you think your partner's feedback was helpful. Why do you think it was helpful or not helpful– someone raise their hand to tell me."

Discuss responses, emphasizing what kind of feedback is helpful. ("You tried to sing too fast and got the movements all mixed up…sing it slower so the movements work better…I like how you kept it simple and sang with good swing feel.")
This activity allows you to continually assess and monitor your students' understanding. You may need to work with your students on how to give helpful feedback if it seems like you are getting responses like "I thought what he did was stupid," etc.

Step 5:

Have partners take turns with responding to CD2-Track 21 one more time without stopping.

Extension:

- Allow partners to perform with CD2-Track 21 in front of class.
- Ask class for feedback on their performances.

Activity 4: Scattin' with the Rhythm Section

CD2-Track 22: Scattin' with the Rhythm Section

(open track mixing in 1, 2, 3 notes, doodle-dah)

"The rhythm section on the recording will play little things that are designed to inspire you to do something with what they give you. For example, they might play rhythms that you can incorporate into your solo. They might play softly at first and then build their accompaniment behind you. You should see if you can mix their ideas into your own improvisation. The rhythm section will help you become a Chop-Monster!"

Step 1:

Play CD2-Track 22 and direct students to do the Chop-Monster Groove while they listen. Ask them to describe some of the things that the rhythm section did, and how they could incorporate those ideas in their solos.

Step 2:

Play CD2-Track 22 again and students should scat sing using three pitches, everyone at the same time, using ideas from the rhythm section on the recording. Repeat as many times as you want.

Step 3:

Ask students to perform their scat with the recording for the class. Ask class for feedback for each singer. Repeat as many times as you want.

🎵 Concert Time

Activity 5: *Feelin' Mighty Hip*

CD-2 Track 23
Feelin' Mighty Hip,
Performance Model, with call-and-response

CD-2 Track 24
Feelin' Mighty Hip,
Backing Track

Step 1:

- Use CD2-Track 23 to model entire song, if you wish. Note that the piano introduction has a characteristic bebop melody, which you'll have fun working up if you plan to play the piano accompaniment in class. Practice the piano accompaniment with CD2-Track 23 or Track 24—you'll find it's easier to play than it looks.
- Teach melody by rote. Students should perform with a hip attitude when singing the hipster lyrics. If you prefer, the melody can be performed a cappella with just a ride cymbal introduction and ride cymbal accompaniment until Orff accompaniment enters at Letter B.
- Use Chop-Monster Moves (waist, shoulders, head) beginning at Letter B/ measure 9/"I'm mighty hip," to represent the three pitches F, A, C.
- Note that for performance, Orff instruments enter at Letter B, and then play through the solo section vamp at Letter C.
- Ride cymbal plays throughout entire arrangement.
- Use backing track, CD2-Track 24, after students have learned their parts.

Melody:

Step 2: Orff Rhythm Section

Divide class and teach rhythm section parts by rote, layering in ride cymbal and Orff parts like you did with *Sticky Situation*. The Orff rhythm section plays as notated below beginning at Letter B, and then repeats their rhythm section pattern throughout the 8-measure vamp at Letter C as they accompany each soloist.

Soprano and alto xylophones ("hi-hat"):

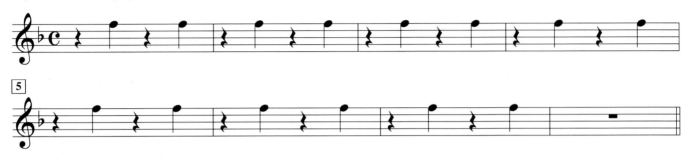

Bass xylophone:

Soprano and alto glockenspiels ("piano"):

Step 3:

Add melody and Chop-Monster Moves to Letter B rhythm section parts.

Step 4:

- Set up in the Scatch-mo Station configuration.
- Begin rhythm section vamp as indicated at letter C.
- Cue soloists to play their improvisations using three notes (F, A, C).   Students should be able to choose how they want to solo. For example, while students are at Station 7 and Station 8:
  - Solos can be two bar call-and-response phrases between students (either echo singing/playing or question and answer).
  - Students can **trade fours** (one person solos for four bars, a second person plays a solo in response for four bars, using elements of the first person's solo as inspiration).
- Students can improvise for the entire 8-bar form of the song.
- Repeat several times through the Scatch-mo Station so everyone gets a chance to play rhythm section parts and improvise.

Step 5: Create an arrangement

Have the class decide on an arrangement. Write choices on the board.
For example:

- Melody can be sung, played on recorders (easier at letter B), played on instruments or rhythm of melody can be played on non-pitched rhythm instruments.
- Rhythm section parts can be played alone or in combinations.
- Improvisations can be sung, played on instruments or done through movement.

Step 6:

- Write the outline of the arrangement on board and have class perform it. (Not musical notation, but a textual roadmap for where the melody will be sung, when the solos will occur and what backgrounds will be played for what solos.)
- Make an audio or video recording of the performance. If you are planning to do Activity 7 (Comparing Two Versions of *Feelin' Mighty Hip*), call this recording, "Feelin' Mighty Hip, Class Recording 1."

Step 7:

Ask students to reflect on the performance. What was good?
What could be better?

Feeling Mighty Hip

The lyrics shown in the score read:

Won-der why I'm grin-nin' from ear to ear?__ 'Cause I'm the hip-pest cat in the hip - is - phere!__

Lyrics (measures 17–21):
Hip-ster, flip-ster, flip-i-ty flip. Feel-in' might-y hip!

C

Open repeat for call & response/solo

Activity 6: Jammin' on *Feelin' Mighty Hip*

Step 1:

Use Scatch-mo Station room setup diagram to set your room up for this activity.
This activity encourages students to be more independent music makers by
creating their own "backing accompaniment" and eventually creating their
own arrangements.

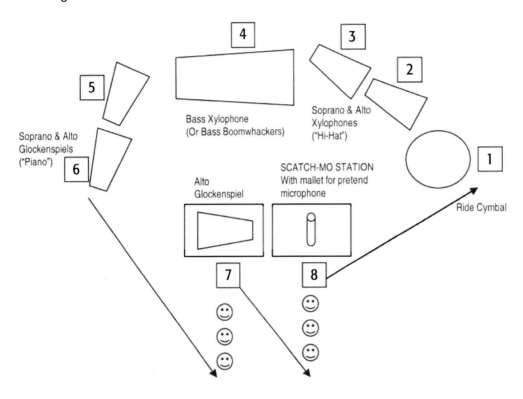

Step 2:

"You are going to improvise or scat sing a 4-bar solo. Before you improvise, you need to choose a **feeling** *that you
want to communicate in your solo, such as sad, happy, hopeful, peaceful, angry, funny and so on. Then, the other
people in your line will try to guess the feeling you were communicating in the next four bars. So, the person at
Station 7 will solo for four bars, and then those in line behind Station 7 will guess the emotion during the next four
measures while the rhythm section keeps playing time. Then the person at the Scatch-mo Station (Station 8) will scat
sing a 4-bar solo and those in line behind their station will guess the emotion they were trying to convey. Then we will
chant 'I'm Hip!' for four measures as we rotate places."*

- Chanting "I'm HIP, I'm HIP" is easy while students rotate places—just emphasize HIP
  on beats 2 & 4.
- Repeat as described above until all students have a turn improvising.
- Write emotions on the board and discuss.

Step 3:

Perform and make a video or audio recording of this more communicative version,
calling it "Feelin' Mighty Hip, Class Recording 2." Be sure to count off each soloist
and say their names on the audio recording so students can guess the emotion
each soloist was portraying—you will need this in order to do Step 4.

Step 4:

Have class listen to their recorded solos. For each solo pause and discuss:
*"What emotion do you think that was? How did they convey that emotion? Let's see if we can guess
the next secret message."*

⊙ Sitting In

The following activities reference resources that are not included with *Chop-Monster Jr.,* such as audio and video recordings and children's literature. We offer these lesson-enrichment ideas to help increase student awareness about the lives and contributions of the great jazz masters.

Link to Jazz Masters: Miles Davis, the Ultimate Hip Cat

Miles Davis (1926–1991)

"Miles Davis was a very cool trumpet player who began his career playing bebop and kept expanding his musical horizons throughout his life. He was so cool that he invented a style of jazz referred to as **cool jazz.** *In this style, he didn't play loud or fast. He kept it simple and swinging. Let's listen to a very hip recording of Miles Davis playing a song called 'Summertime,' composed by George Gershwin. What do you think you are going to hear? Will the instruments sound loud or soft? Will the tempo be slow or fast?"*

Miles Davis

Courtesy of the Institute of Jazz Studies

Teacher's Guide to Listening Activity

Miles Davis, the Ultimate Hip Cat

CD-2
Track 25

Listening: Summertime

Use our recording of "Summertime" on Track 25, or locate a recording of Miles Davis's rendition of George Gershwin's "Summertime," as recorded on his legendary album *Porgy and Bess* (Columbia/Legacy).

Reproducible Worksheet/Transparency Master 3: Jazz Performers

Step 1: Listen

- Display Worksheet/Transparency Master 3: Jazz Performers and identify Miles Davis.
- Play a recording of "Summertime" from Miles Davis, *Porgy and Bess.* Or, use our cool jazz version on Track 25, making sure you inform students that it is not Miles Davis playing, but is another trumpet player, Justin Ray, performing in a cool jazz style.
- While listening, have students do the Chop-Monster Groove, chant the doodle-dah rhythm or demonstrate kneedle-dah movement to the recording, and reflect on how easy it is for them now.

Step 2: Talk about the recording

"How do you feel on a really hot day in the summer? If you were sitting outside, would you be running around playing games or sitting still in the shade? How does Miles Davis communicate that feeling in his solo?"

Tip from Kim

Miles Davis's cool jazz music is accessible for elementary school children. His recording of "Summertime" is ideal because the improvised solos are relatively short and stay close to the melody. He emotes an intensity of feeling that is easy to grasp. The tempo is slow enough that children can clearly feel a steady beat, beats 2 & 4 played by the drummer's hi-hat, and feel the triplet undertow of the swing eighth notes. Use this music anytime to lead kids into your room or line them up to leave; it's always a popular choice!

Link to Literature

Lookin' for Bird in the Big City

Read aloud *Lookin' for Bird in the Big City*, Robert Burleigh, illustrations by Marek Los (Silver Whistle Harcourt, Inc.). It is a story about Miles Davis coming to New York when he was still a teenager to find and learn from Charlie Parker. This story is what might have happened to Miles Davis as he looked for Bird (Charlie Parker). This book helps support the message that jazz takes practice and even great musicians like Miles Davis had to work at becoming great musicians.

Optional: Read along to a recording of "So What" included on *Ken Burns Jazz: The Story of America's Music,* Disc 4.

Hip Cat

Read *Hip Cat* by Jonathan London, illustrated by Woodleigh Hubbard. (Chronicle Books). In this book, a character named Hip Cat journeys to the city by the bay to live his dream of being a jazz musician. Hip Cat wears a beret, reminiscent of Dizzy Gillespie. The book encourages young people to work at what they love to the best of their ability. It is dedicated to the memory of Miles Davis and John Coltrane, another jazz innovator.

Optional: Read along to recordings included on *Ken Burns Jazz: The Story of America's Music,* Disc 3, beginning with "Straight, No Chaser" followed by "Manteca."

"What do you think Hip Cat's music would sound like? Who do you think the creators of Hip Cat might have modeled Hip Cat after?"

Dizzy Gillespie, Charlie Parker and Miles Davis (and John Coltrane)

Video: *Hip Cat* Reading Rainbow Episode 127

Extension:

Play the *Hip Cat Reading Rainbow Video* (Episode 127) that shows the jazz group playing in the club. This great video breaks down the instruments of the rhythm section so students can really see what they all look like and how they are played. (Reading Rainbow, 1997. GPN Program number 126.127.)

"Compared to the recordings we have listened to so far, which do you think Hip Cat's group on the video sounds the most like? Why?"

There is not one "right" answer because there are influences from all the jazz masters in this video recording. For example, they use instruments like Charlie Parker and Dizzy Gillespie used in their bebop groups, they swing like Count Basie, etc.

Link to History

Jazz: A Film by Ken Burns
"All Blues" or "So What," Miles Davis. Episode 9, *Jazz: A Film by Ken Burns,*
(PBS Home Video)
www.pbs.org/jazz

Jazz for Young People Curriculum
Lesson 15, *Jazz for Young People Curriculum*, Marsalis, 2002, Jazz at Lincoln Center,
compact disc/teacher's guide/student guide.
www.jazzatlincolncenter.org

Websites:

Official Miles Davis Website
Includes authorized photographs, a video clip of "All Blues" and sound clips of
"Summertime" and "So What."
www.milesdavis.com/home.htm

Ken Burns Jazz Kids
The "Now and Then" portion of this website features a good biography
of Miles Davis.
www.pbs.org/jazz/kids/nowthen/miles.html

Ken Burns Jazz
Ken Burns Jazz features a lengthy biography of Miles Davis.
www.pbs.org/jazz/biography/artist_id_davis_miles.htm

The Art of Miles Davis
Authorized site for visual art created by Miles Davis.
www.comptoncassey.demon.co.uk/

The Jazz Files
Photos and sound clips of Miles Davis recordings on this jazz tribute site.
www.thejazzfiles.com/JazzDavis.html

 reedom in Jazz

- Major and minor chords
- Making the changes

Preparing for Success

✓ Jam Session

Students will demonstrate through movement, scat singing and playing instruments that they hear major and minor chords and can improvise to them.

Activity 1: Jazzy Chords
Activity 2: Movin' to Jazzy Chords
Activity 3: Scat Singing to the Changes
Activity 4: Making the Changes
Activity 5: *Dogs and Cats,* Orff Version
Activity 6: *Dogs and Cats,* Jazz Band Version with open improvisation section
Link: Benny Goodman

Vocabulary

Chord, major, minor, making the changes

Materials

- *Chop-Monster Jr.* CD2-Tracks 26–32
- Worksheet 14: How Did I Do? Rubric
- Ride cymbal with drumstick
- Low pitched drum with soft mallet (e.g., large hand drum, roto-tom, tom-tom)
- Alto glockenspiel with 2 mallets (A)
- "Dogs" Alto Glockenspiel (D, F♯, A, B)
- "Cats" Alto Glockenspiel (D, F, A, B)
- Soprano and alto xylophone with 2 mallets (D)
- Bass xylophone with 2 mallets (D, A, B, A) or D, A, B, A bass Boomwhackers

Indicators of Success

Students demonstrate through movement and playing that they hear minor and major chords.

Students scat sing and play short responses to singer's calls using major and minor thirds.

♪ Concert Time

Students will have a major and minor chord "battle of the bands" performance with *Dogs and Cats* using Orff and rhythm instruments.

⊙ Sitting In

Students will learn about Benny Goodman and His Orchestra through suggested learning links to literature and recordings.

Unless specified, you will need to supply the referenced audio or video recordings.

Link to Jazz Masters

"Sing, Sing, Sing," Louis Prima. *Sing, Sing, Sing,* Benny Goodman and His Orchestra, RCABluebird, audio recording.
www.bluebirdjazz.com

"Sing, Sing, Sing," is also featured on Disc 2, *Ken Burns Jazz: The Story of America's Music,* Columbia/Legacy 5-CD set, audio recording.
www.legacyrecordings.com

Link to Literature

Once Upon a Time in Chicago: The Story of Benny Goodman, Jonah Winter, pictures by Jeanette Winter. New York: Hyperion Books for Children, 2000.
www.disney.go.com/disneybooks/hyperionbooks

The Sound that Jazz Makes, Carole Boston Weatherford, illustrated by Eric Velasquez. New York: Walker and Company, 2000.
www.walkerbooks.com

Link to History

Jazz: A Film by Ken Burns, Episode 5, Florentine Films/PBS/Warner Home Video, 2000, 10-episode video series (also DVD).
www.pbs.org/jazz

Jazz for Young People Curriculum, Lesson 6, Marsalis, New York: Jazz at Lincoln Center, 2002, teaching curriculum with 30 student guides, 10-CD set audio recordings and video recording.
www.jazzatlincolncenter.org

✓ Jam Session

Introduction

"You have improvised using one, two and three pitches and using doodle-dah and swing feel. You have played instruments or body percussion to create a rhythm section. You have also listened and compared your versions of songs to different versions performed by the jazz group on the CD.

*"All of your improvising has occurred on one **chord**. A chord is three or more notes played at the same time. Chords combine together to create a full and harmonious sound, which makes the melody sound more interesting. Chords add color! Instruments such as piano and guitar can play three or more notes at a time so we often think of them as harmony instruments. When you have combined all of your parts together, you have also been creating **chords**! Let's see how this works."*

Note: *Chop-Monster Jr.* does not teach chords in context of diatonic harmony. The goal of this activity is to train students to hear the difference between major and minor chord "colors" by changing one note: lowering the "middle" note of their hip three-note scat singing (the major 3rd) to a lower middle note (the minor 3rd). Alfred Publishing offers two improvisation tutors for further study, *Chop-Monster 1* and *Chop-Monster 2,* which teach diatonic jazz harmony, the blues and more advanced jazz concepts.

Activity 1: Jazzy Chords

CD-2

 Track 26

Two chords
(D major triad and D minor triad)

Step 1:

"You will hear the jazz group on the recording play two different chords. When you hear the chords change, quickly raise your hand and just as quickly pull your hand back down."

- This may be challenging the first time, but that is fine. The steps in this activity will lead them to hear exactly when the chords change, and the final step is to repeat this listening activity to see how developed their ears have become. In this way, children will be confident that they can "make the changes" when it's time to perform the last piece in the book.
- Before playing CD2-Track 26, have students practice putting their hands up fast and pulling them down fast. You don't want them sitting with their hands up for 8 or 16 bars so it's important they understand to put their hands up and down fast. Practice this by saying "change, change, change" as they put their hands up and down.
- Play CD2-Track 26, and observe how well students can hear the chords change.

"Who can tell me about what they hear in the two different chords?"

Give students ample time to reflect and answer.

Tip from Margaret:

You might notice students looking around to see when the others raise their hands for the chord change the first few times. Some will put their hands up because other kids do. A way to make sure students are independently making decisions is to ask them to close their eyes during the activity.

CD-2
Track 27 **Major chord (D)**

Step 2:

"Now listen to a different recording, which we'll call Example A."

> Play CD2-Track 27. It has the same feel and tempo but stays on one chord (D major).

"How did that sound? What mood did it sound like to you?"

- Look for answers that identify the music as staying on one chord, and answers that describe the mood (happy, content, positive) or "color" (warm, bright, sunny).
- Give time for students to think after you ask questions. It may take them a little while to figure out how to put what they are thinking in words.
- Identify that musicians call this kind of chord a **major chord**.

Step 3: Add movement

> Sing the notes of the D major triad as you lead a movement activity as follows:
> On the note D, put hands on waist
> On the note F♯, put hands on shoulders
> On the note A, put hands on head
> Sing with syllables such as *do, mi, sol* or *1, 3, 5* or *low, middle, high*—whatever system you prefer.
> Lead activity in "Simon says" fashion and see how well students can sing the pitches on their own.
> Then group children in three parts and cue D, F♯, and A. Have students hold their note so they can hear that they are singing a D major triad.

CD-2
Track 28 **Minor triad (Dm)**

Step 4:

"Now listen to a recording which we'll call Example B."

> Play CD2-Track 28. It has a similar feel and tempo, but stays on the F minor triad.

"How did that sound different? What mood or color did it sound like to you?"

> Look for answers that describe the mood or color (sad, thoughtful, quiet, cool, blue). After ample reflection and discussion time, identify that musicians call this kind of chord a **minor chord.**

Step 5: Add movement

> Sing the notes of the D minor triad as you lead a movement activity:
> On the note D, put hands on waist.
> On the note F (natural), put hands on opposite shoulders and tell children they are hugging the minor note, the sad note (or whatever mood description your students have come up with). Inflect your voice with the minor mood your students want to portray.
> On the note A, put hands on head.
> Sing with syllables such as *do, me, sol* or *1, flat-3, 5* or *D, F, A* or *low, hug, high*—whatever system you prefer.
> Lead activity in "Simon says" fashion and see how well students can sing the pitches on their own.
> Then group children in three parts, and cue D, F, and A so students are singing a D minor triad.

CD-2
Track 26

Two chords again

Step 6:

"Listen again to the recording. There are two chords that change. We'll call it Example C this time. Close your eyes as you listen and put your hands up and down when you hear the major and minor chords change."

> Play CD2-Track 26 again and observe more confident identification when chords change.

"Which example sounded most interesting to you? Let's say you were going to improvise to Example A, B or C—which example would you want to jam with? Why? What was it about that one that hooked your ears?"

Activity 2: Movin' to Jazzy Chords

CD-2
Track 29

Jazzy Chords
(with scat singing)

"Let's listen to a different recording that has both major and minor chords in it. Let's add some movement that will demonstrate that we can hear when the chords change. Walk in one direction in a circle for the first chord, the major chord. When you hear the second chord, the minor chord, bend over, change directions and walk in the opposite direction. Then when you hear the major chord again, stand up and walk in the original direction, and so on."

> Play CD2-Track 29 and lead the circle activity. Students should be standing and walking during the major chord and bending over and walking in the opposite direction during the minor chord.

*"You have just done what jazz musicians call **making the changes**. You can hear when the chords change—that means you are developing some monster ears!"*

Activity 3: Scat Singing on the Changes

CD-2
Track 29

Call-and-Response to the Changes
(same track as Movin' to Jazzy Chords)

Step 1: Call-and-Response

"You can make the changes, so now we are going to echo sing with the CD. Let's listen to the track first and do the Chop-Monster Groove. See if you can hear the singer making the changes."

> Play CD2-Track 29. Listen and do the groove.
> Repeat and have students echo the singer.
> Repeat until students are imitating the singer's inflections exactly.
> Ask for volunteers (either in pairs or solo) to demonstrate their echo singing chops.

Step 2: Improvise

"Let's try it again and this time when you respond, improvise a different phrase that works with the changes. Hum your responses to yourself for now as you try out your ideas. As you practice, see if you can put some of the interesting vocal inflections you hear the singer make into your response."

- Play CD2-Track 29. Students improvise all at the same time, humming their responses to themselves.
- Repeat this many times while you walk around your students so you can hear each one sing. This will help you to know when most of the children are solid with the activity.

Tip From Margaret

> Whenever you sense the students are a little shy about singing something new like this you can have them hum quietly to themselves first.

**Call-and-Response
to Two Chords**

Play CD2-Track 29 again and ask for students to hold up one finger if they want to improvise an answer to the singer's call. That way you can call on those who feel the most confident. Give lots of praise, have the class applaud after each small solo.

Activity 4: Making the Changes on Instruments

Create your own audio or video recording

This activity does not use a CD track; students create their own groove.

Set up rhythm section with cymbal and Orff instruments (see Dogs and Cats Room Setup, but don't refer to the two improvising groups as Dogs and Cats yet; just call them groups one and two or stations 7 and 8.)

Step 1: Rhythm section swing groove

"We're going to improvise and make the changes on our instruments. Before we can jam, we need to get our swing groove going with the rhythm section."

Have rhythm section students create a simple rhythm section swing groove in 4/4:
- Ride Cymbal—swing eighth-note groove (gum, bubble gum)
- Alto xylophone or short A boomwhacker—beats 2 & 4 for hi-hat effect.
- Bass xylophone or bass Boomwhacker—steady beat on D.
- Alto glockenspiel—half notes on A.

The rhythm section swing groove will not imply a major or minor tonality—improvising students will choose in their solos how they want to make the changes in Step 2.

Step 2: Improvise and make the changes

"Your solo is a personal way of describing how you are feeling now, or how you felt in the past. If you have no huge feeling now, remember a feeling you had before—such as how it feels to open a really great birthday present, or how it feels when you are too tired to stay awake for a favorite TV show. Or, remember a story or experience that gave you a certain feeling that you would like to share with everybody through music."

- Prompt discussion about feelings they may have had in the past, such as:
  - Crashing on their bike
  - Drinking something nice and cool on a really hot day
  - Hitting a home run
  - Being scared in the dark
- Line up two groups of students behind Stations 7 and 8 to take turns playing barred instruments for their solos.
- You can either have Station 7 improvise "major chord" feelings using the three notes of the D major chord (use bars D, F♯, A), and Station 8 improvise "minor chord" feelings using the three notes of the D minor chord (use bars D, F, A). Or, have students decide which type of chord they will imply through their improvisations, and have other students guess the feeling they are trying to communicate.
- Their solos should freely incorporate jazz phrases they tried in Activity 3—they should "speak" with the jazz language they have been learning.
- Their solos can be two, four or eight bars in length.

Step 3: *Prepare to record the performance.*

Video recording is a fun option at this point because by now kids are showing natural movement to the swing feel by bobbing heads, etc.

"Think of two different feelings/moods/stories or emotions that you want to express using the D major chord and the D minor chord you have been practicing. Come up with two moods that are opposites such as happy/sad, hyper/sleepy, lonely/having fun with friends, sharing a secret/keeping a secret. Someone who listens to you, who doesn't speak your language, should be able to identify their feelings through the music you are playing—it should be very obvious."

- Give students some quiet time to think about their opposite moods.
- When they are ready they should hold up one finger to let you know they have come up with their ideas, remaining quiet while others are thinking.
- Once the class is ready, practice first before recording– layer in the rhythm section, then cue improvisers to play their opposite moods. Practice rotating through Stations 1 through 8.
- Everyone gets to improvise on an instrument and play each part in the rhythm section during the station rotation. There will be no breaks because students will already know how to move through the stations (as they rotate through stations, have them chant a swing pattern they have learned such as "Let's swing, let's swing, keep it going, make it swing.")

Step 4: *It's time to JAM!*

- Have students name their masterpiece. Whatever they come up with could be added at the beginning of the video with the whole class pictured saying something like, "Presenting Mr. Clark's 5th grade class, jammin' out in 'Clarks' Coolness!'" If you create an audio recording, you can have them say this into the recorder.
- You could share the recording with other classes with the understanding that if one class watches another, the other class will also watch yours.
- Say "recording" to alert students you are starting the video or audio recorder, and have students perform their masterpiece, rotating through the rhythm section and improvisation stations.
- Playback your recording and enjoy!

Extension:

Have students evaluate themselves using the "How did I do?" rubric. Before the jam, students and you should decide on what they should be able to do on all parts and solos to get a "Fabulous," "OK," or "I need to woodshed." The students should write the target areas in the "questions" boxes before doing the activity. Have students turn in assessments so you can see the ratings each child gave themselves. This will tell you how well students are able to hear and comment correctly on their own performances.

🎵 Concert Time

Activity 6 / *Dogs and Cats*

CD-2
Tracks 30–32

CD2-Track 30: *Dogs and Cats,* **Performance Model, with call-and-response**

CD2-Track 31: *Dogs and Cats,* **Backing Track, with open solo section**

CD2-Track 32: *Dogs and Cats,* **Jazz Band Arrangement, with open solo section**

"Some jazz concerts feature two big bands in a fun contest they call a 'battle of the bands.' We're going to have our own fun concert, performing a song where we pretend that we are dogs and cats—and the dogs claim they *are the best, and the cats claim* they *are the best. When we get to the solo section of the song, the dogs are going to improvise to a major chord, and the cats are going to improvise to a minor chord."*

Step 1: Teach Melody

Teach *Dogs and Cats* melody by rote. Make note of the minor 3rd in the Cat part.

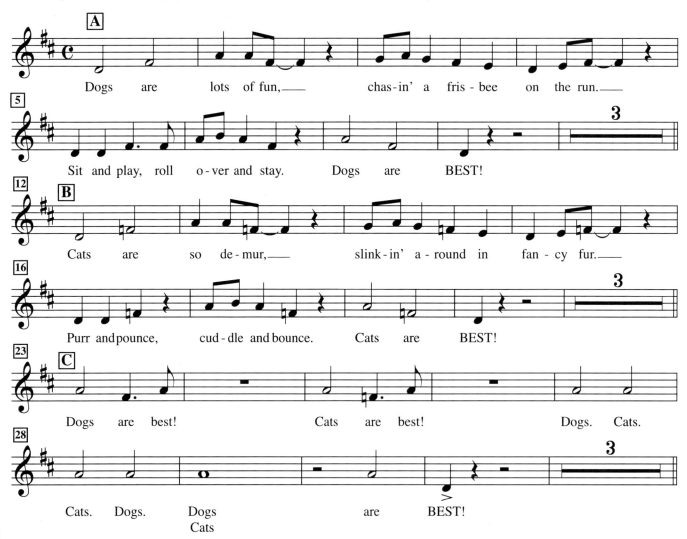

Step 2:

Divide class into two groups: the Dogs and the Cats. Have the two groups face each other by kneeling across from each other (longways). All of the dogs will be on one side and all of the cats will be on the opposite side, facing each other.

Step 3:

Teach the song parts again, cueing dogs to sing only when it is the "dog part" and cats to sing only in the "cat part." They will sing together at the end of the melody, so make sure they say their respective "dog" or "cat" lyric when the lyrics say "Dogs/Cats are the best!"

CD-2
Track 30

Dogs and Cats, **Performance Model,**
with call-and-response

Step 4: Call-and-Response

Have students perform *Dogs and Cats* melody with CD2-Track 30, which is a performance model with a call-and-response section. Cue each side when its time to sing their part.

Note that the introduction features four measures of tom-tom, playing the "gum bubble gum" swing eighth pattern students have been playing on the ride cymbal. This is reminiscent of the introduction to Benny Goodman's hit, "Sing, Sing, Sing." At letter D, there is a call-and-response section on the recorded track (open for improvised solos in the backing track CD2-Track 31 and in the Orff arrangement): eight measures of a D major triad where the dogs will echo sing, and eight measures of the D minor triad where the cats will echo sing.

CD-2
Track 31

Dogs and Cats, **Backing Track,**
with open solo section

Step 5: Improvise to Backing Track

Have students perform *Dogs and Cats* using backing track, CD2-Track 31, taking turns scat singing and "making the changes" during the open solo section (at letter D).

Step 6: Teach Orff arrangement

- Set up room as shown in *Dogs and Cats* Room Setup Diagram.
- Students will eventually rotate parts much like they did with the Scatch-mo Station.
- If you are teaching younger students, you may want to split the tom-tom/cymbal part between two players, in which case you will need to position two students at Station One (one on tom-tom, one on ride cymbal).
- If you don't have a tom-tom, substitute a large hand drum, roto-tom, or any other suitable drum.
- Students have played all of the rhythms in previous arrangements, so transferring parts from body percussion is optional.

Dog Part—Orff instruments, measures 5–12 (letter A)

- Bass—Teach bass xylophone part beginning at Letter A (measures 5–12), or split part among three bass Boomwhacker players (D, A, B with octivator caps).
- Ride Cymbal—layer on top of bass line.
- Hi-hat—Add soprano xylophone part ("D" on beats 2 & 4).
- Piano—Teach alto xylophone and glockenspiel parts.
- Combine bass xylophone, cymbal, "hi-hat" and "piano" to create a swinging rhythm section playing the D major groove.
- Have dog group sing their melody.

Cat Part—Orff instruments, measures 16–23 (letter B)

- The only part that changes is the alto xylophone part, which plays an F natural to create the minor chord sound (instead of an F sharp).
- Combine all parts and have cat group sing their melody.

Dog/Cat Part—Orff instruments, measures 27–35 (letter C)

- Teach parts by rote at Letter C, again encouraging students to listen carefully and make the changes. Combine all parts and have dogs and cats sing together.

Improvisation Section—Orff parts, measures 39–54 (letter D)
- This section is 16 measures, combining letters A and B into a two-chord vamp. Improvisers will take turns in their groups, each playing an 8-bar solo with their three notes (D, F♯, A or D, F, A). The dogs will improvise during the D major triad section on their barred instrument, and the cats will improvise during the D minor triad section. Students will easily hear when the chords change.

Putting it All Together
- Teach the tom-tom introduction and practice the entire song form with the tom-tom breaks. If you choose to rotate the rhythm section parts, the tom-tom part can be performed with the entire class clapping hands to the rhythm as they move to new stations. Or, assign one person to always play the tom-tom.
- Practice the vamp ending, again encouraging creative scat singing with dog and cat sound effects.
- It is important that students memorize their parts, so they are internalizing the music and hearing when the chords change. Do not write out their parts or make copies of the teacher's score.

Dogs and Cats Room Setup Diagram

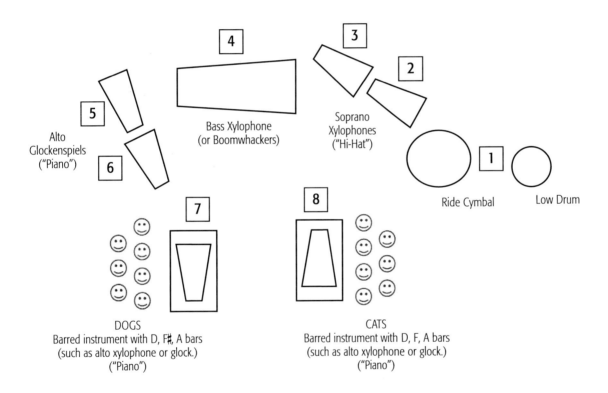

Step 6: Extension

Have students create their own arrangement (e.g., different non-pitched instruments to play hi-hat part; play the soprano/alto glockenspiel part on a real piano, experiment with different drums for tom-toms, etc.).
Record their performance and use guiding questions to have students reflect on their performance.

Perform again, incorporating suggestions the class made.
Continue with reflection following performance of their new and improved performance (with or without a recording, depending on how well the students recall what happened in their arrangement).

Dogs and Cats

"Dogs" sing @ LetterA
"Cats" sing @ Letter B
"Dogs" and "Cats" sing @ Letter C

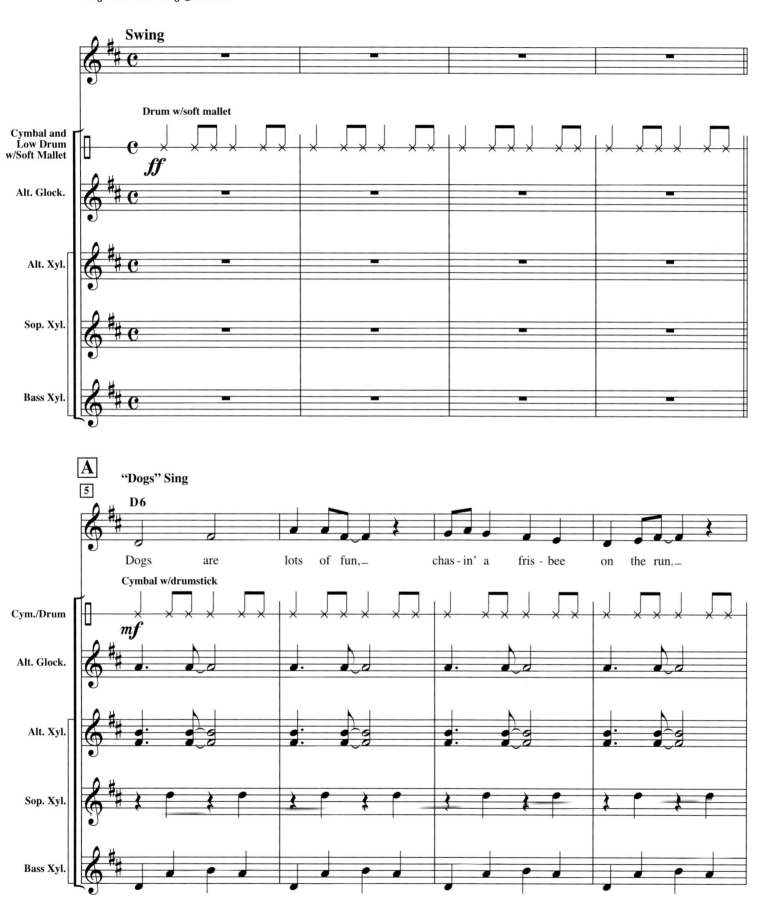

Dogs are lots of fun,— chas-in' a fris-bee on the run.—

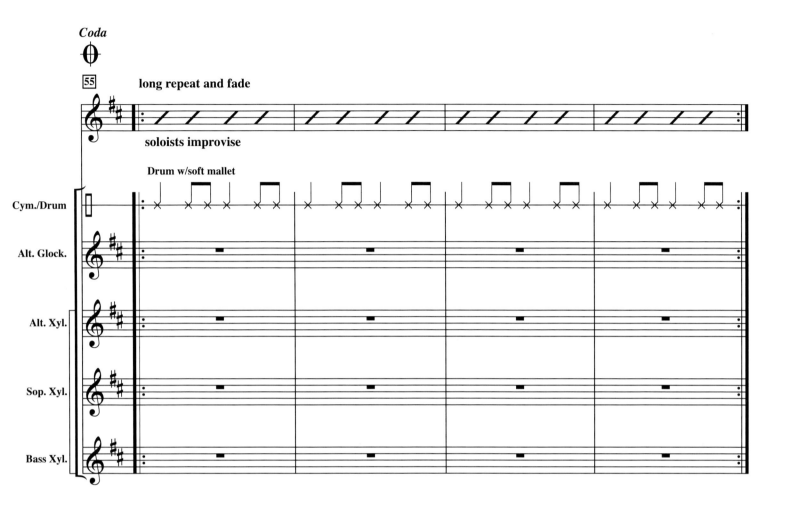

Activity 6 / *Dogs and Cats* Jazz Band Version (with open solo section)

CD-2
Track 32 ***Dogs and Cats* Jazz Band Version,**
with open solo section

- This activity gives students the opportunity to improvise with a jazz band accompaniment.
- Have students listen to CD2-Track 32, *Dogs and Cats* jazz band arrangement and compare it to the Orff arrangement that they played.
- Ask questions that guide students to identify the way the music swings, the way the bass is played (legato, walking), and the way the saxophone, trombone and trumpet sections phrase together and use characteristic jazz language. See if they can identify when the chords change in the open solo section.
- Have students take turns improvising to the D major chord and the D minor chord in the open solo section.
- Make a video recording of your grand finale performance.

☺ Sitting In

The following activities reference resources that are not included with *Chop-Monster Jr.*, such as audio and video recordings and children's literature. We offer these lesson-enrichment ideas to help increase student awareness about the lives and contributions of the great jazz masters.

Link to Jazz Masters: Stomping with Benny Goodman

Benny Goodman (1909–1986)

"Benny Goodman was born in 1909 in a tough neighborhood of Chicago. His parents had settled there after escaping from Russia during the 'progroms,' which were attacks on people of Jewish heritage. Benny learned to play the clarinet, and soon formed his own bands. He led a popular big band in the 1930s until his death in 1986, and was also famous for his small groups.

"Benny was one of the first white jazz musicians to break an old unwritten rule against black and white musicians playing together in the same band. Benny helped to change that practice by asking black pianist Teddy Wilson and later black vibraphonist Lionel Hampton to play in his small group with drummer Gene Krupa. Benny helped people to understand that there should be no rules about who can play with whom in jazz. He even asked pianist Mary Lou Williams to write songs his band. In those days, women were also rare in jazz groups.

"Benny Goodman became so popular, the media nicknamed him the King of Swing. One of the most famous 'battle of the bands' occurred in 1937 between the Benny Goodman Orchestra and the Chick Webb Orchestra (featuring Ella Fitzgerald). Listen to the great Benny Goodman Orchestra play one of their big hits, called 'Sing, Sing, Sing'."

Teacher's Guide to Listening Activity

Stomping with Benny Goodman

Courtesy of the Institute of Jazz Studies

Listening: Sing, Sing, Sing

Locate a recording of "Sing, Sing, Sing" by Louis Prima, recorded by the Benny Goodman Orchestra. It is featured in the 5-CD set, *Ken Burns Jazz, The Story of America's Music* (Columbia/Legacy), among others. Note the exciting drums throughout, the swinging rhythms and the great ensemble playing. The National Public Radio lists "Sing, Sing, Sing" on its list of 100 most important American musical works of the 20th century.

Other Benny Goodman Orchestra recordings that are great for children to listen to are "King Porter Stomp," and "Stompin' at the Savoy."

Link to Literature

Once Upon a Time in Chicago

Read aloud *Once Upon a Time in Chicago: The Story of Benny Goodman* by Jonah Winter, pictures by Jeanette Winter (Hyperion). This storybook tells about a poor Jewish boy growing up in Chicago, wanting to play the clarinet, and how his family struggled to make his dream come true.

Benny Goodman

Optional: Read along to recordings included on *Ken Burns Jazz: The Story of America's Music,* Disc 2, beginning with "King Porter Stomp" followed by "Rose Room."

Link to History

Jazz: A Film by Ken Burns
Episode 5, *Jazz: A Film by Ken Burns*, PBS Home Video, 2001, DVD/videocassette.
www.pbs.org/jazz

Jazz for Young People Curriculum
Lesson 6, *Jazz for Young People Curriculum*, Marsalis, New York: Jazz at Lincoln Center, 2002, compact discs/teacher's guide/student guides.
www.jazzatlincolncenter.org

Ken Burns Jazz Kids
The "Now and Then" section features a short biography of Benny Goodman.
www.pbs.org/jazz/kids/nowthen/goodman.html

Ken Burns Jazz
An extended biography of Benny Goodman is featured on this website.
www.pbs.org/jazz/biography/artist_id_goodman_benny.htm

VH1 Benny Goodman Web Page
Another good biography of Benny Goodman is featured here.
http://www.vh1.com/artists/az/goodman_benny/bio.jhtml

Optional Literature Extension

The Sound That Jazz Makes
As a follow up to *Chop-Monster Jr.*, read aloud *The Sound That Jazz Makes* by Carole Boston Weatherford, illustrated by Eric Velasquez (Walker and Company). This is a nice overview of the history of jazz, connecting the roots of jazz through different styles of jazz, to the last page that says "JAZZ is a downbeat born in our nation, chords of struggle and jubilation, bursting forth from hearts set free in notes that echo history. This is the sound that jazz makes!"

Optional: After reading the book, play "The History of Jazz According to Mary Lou" from the compact disc by Mary Lou Williams *Live at the Keystone Korner* (Highnote HCD 7097).

Congratulations!

Upon completion of this activity, your students have graduated from Chop-Monster Jr.

During this course of study your young students have developed good listening chops—plus some monster jazz skills such as making the changes, scat singing and improvising their feelings to chords. They have also learned about legendary jazz masters and have expanded their understanding of a wonderful musical art form—JAZZ.

We hope you will continue to expand your students' musical horizons and listen to more jazz yourself as the rest of the year unfolds. To learn more about teaching jazz, we encourage you to join IAJE– the International Association for Jazz Education (www.iaje.org)–and explore its numerous educational outreach programs.

With sincere appreciation,

Shelly Berg   Margaret Fitzgerald   Kimberly McCord

Worksheet 1: Musical Instruments in Jazz

Full Name _____

Saxophone

Guitar

Trombone

Trumpet

Piano

Clarinet

Drums

Bass

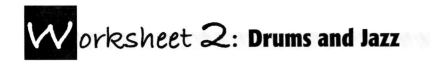
Worksheet 2: Drums and Jazz

Full Name _____

Oh, Lady Be Good
Words and music by George Gershwin and Ira Gershwin

Questions for First Listening	The Eureka Brass Band	Jones-Smith Incorporated
1. *Where* do you think a band that sounds like this would perform?		
2. What kinds of *percussion instruments* do you hear?		
Questions for Second Listening	**The Eureka Brass Band**	**Jones-Smith Incorporated**
1. What is the *same* about the drums in both recordings?		
2. What is *different*?		
3. Listen to the *cymbal parts* in each version of the song and *describe* what you hear.		
4. One of these groups sounds more like a jazz group than the other. Put an "X" in the box under the group that sounds the *most* like jazz.		

Worksheet 3: Jazz Masters

Full Name _____

Louis Armstrong

Duke Ellington

Mary Lou Williams

Ella Fitzgerald

Count Basie

Benny Goodman

Dizzy Gillespie

Charlie Parker

Miles Davis

Full Name _____

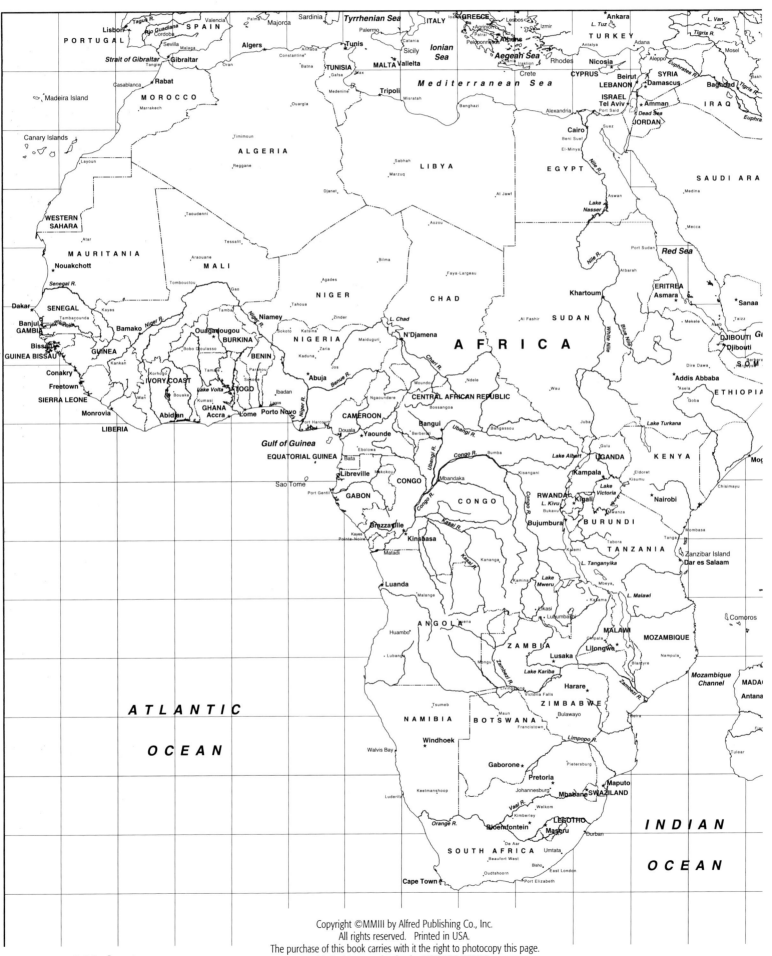

orksheet 5: Rockin' Chair Listening Map

Full Name _____

Rockin' Chair
Words and music by Hoagy Carmichael
Recorded by Louis Armstrong and Jack Teagarden

Introduction played by_____

FIRST LISTEN	SECOND LISTEN
Vocals First Time	**Vocals First Time**
Vocals Second Time	**Vocals Second Time**
Conversation between trumpet and trombone	**Conversation between trumpet and trombone**
Bonus question: What is he doing to the flies around the old rockin' chair?	

Worksheet 6: Take the "A" Train Listening Map

Full Name _____

Take the "A" Train
Words and music by Billy Strayhorn
Recorded by Duke Ellington and His Orchestra, Carmen Bradford, and many others

Piano Intro

Melody Car

★ =(A) *You must take the "A" train, to go to Sugar Hill way up in Harlem.* □
★ =(A) *If you miss the "A" train, you'll find you missed the quickest way to Harlem.* □
○ =(B) *Hurry, get on, now it's coming. Listen to those rails a-humming. All aboard,* □
★ =(A) *Get on the "A" train. Soon you will be on Sugar Hill in Harlem.*

Solo Car

Start

End

Fun Car

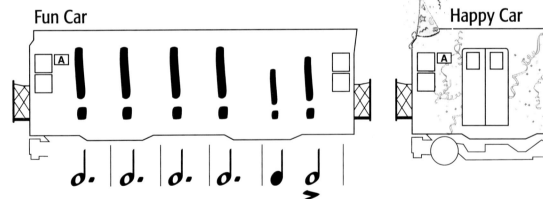

Happy Car

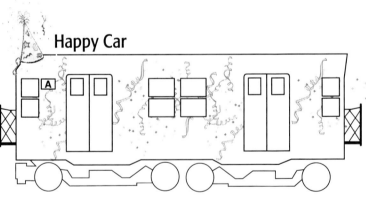

Melody Car

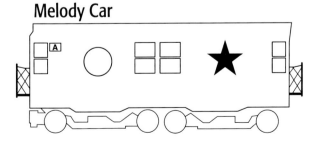

Softer

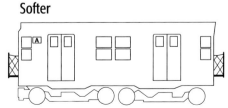

Softest

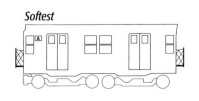

Worksheet 7: Thinking About Improvisation

(Two-sided/Two pages) **Side A**

Full Name _____

	Terrific	OK	Needs Work	Terrific	OK	Needs Work	Terrific	OK	Needs Work	Terrific	OK	Needs Work
Group A	Singer 1			Singer 2			Singer 3			Singer 4		
Solo was interesting to listen to												
Solo stayed on one note												
Solo sounded like jazz												
Comments?												

	Terrific	OK	Needs Work	Terrific	OK	Needs Work	Terrific	OK	Needs Work	Terrific	OK	Needs Work
Group B	Singer 1			Singer 2			Singer 3			Singer 4		
Solo was interesting to listen to												
Solo stayed on one note												
Solo sounded like jazz												
Comments?												

	Terrific	OK	Needs Work	Terrific	OK	Needs Work	Terrific	OK	Needs Work	Terrific	OK	Needs Work
Group C	Singer 1			Singer 2			Singer 3			Singer 4		
Solo was interesting to listen to												
Solo stayed on one note												
Solo sounded like jazz												
Comments?												

	Terrific	OK	Needs Work	Terrific	OK	Needs Work	Terrific	OK	Needs Work	Terrific	OK	Needs Work
Group D	Singer 1			Singer 2			Singer 3			Singer 4		
Solo was interesting to listen to												
Solo stayed on one note												
Solo sounded like jazz												
Comments?												

Worksheet 7: Thinking About Improvisation

(Two-sided/Two pages) **Side B**

Full Name _____

	Terrific	OK	Needs Work	Terrific	OK	Needs Work	Terrific	OK	Needs Work	Terrific	OK	Needs Work
Group E	**Singer 1**			**Singer 2**			**Singer 3**			**Singer 4**		
Solo was interesting to listen to												
Solo stayed on one note												
Solo sounded like jazz												
Comments?												

	Terrific	OK	Needs Work	Terrific	OK	Needs Work	Terrific	OK	Needs Work	Terrific	OK	Needs Work
Group F	**Singer 1**			**Singer 2**			**Singer 3**			**Singer 4**		
Solo was interesting to listen to												
Solo stayed on one note												
Solo sounded like jazz												
Comments?												

	Terrific	OK	Needs Work	Terrific	OK	Needs Work	Terrific	OK	Needs Work	Terrific	OK	Needs Work
Group G	**Singer 1**			**Singer 2**			**Singer 3**			**Singer 4**		
Solo was interesting to listen to												
Solo stayed on one note												
Solo sounded like jazz												
Comments?												

	Terrific	OK	Needs Work	Terrific	OK	Needs Work	Terrific	OK	Needs Work	Terrific	OK	Needs Work
Group H	**Singer 1**			**Singer 2**			**Singer 3**			**Singer 4**		
Solo was interesting to listen to												
Solo stayed on one note												
Solo sounded like jazz												
Comments?												

Worksheet 8: How High the Moon Listening Map

Full Name _____

How High the Moon

Words and music by Nancy Hamilton and Morgan Lewis
Recorded by Ella Fitzgerald, Carmen Bradford, and many others

(INTRODUCTION)

(VERSE 1 AND VERSE 2)

Name the instruments you hear playing:

_____

_____

Did the instruments drown out the singing? (circle one)   Yes   No

If "No," why didn't the instruments overpower the singing?

_____

(DRUM BREAK) SOLO

Bonus question:
What happens to the TEMPO here?

_____

(VERSE 3 AND VERSE 4) Listen and write down six "scat" syllables
that you like or find interesting on the recording, such as "Boo-Dee":

_____

_____

_____

How does Ella Fitzgerald's (or Carmen Bradford's) voice sound to you? Does she make her voice sound
like anything you've already heard? (Maybe an instrument?)

Describe:

_____

_____

Worksheet 9: Got Chops? Thinking About Improvisation

Full Name _____

	Partner 1	Partner 2
Were the solos interesting to listen to? Why or why not?		
Did the solos have a feeling that was expressed to the listeners?		
What ideas did you hear in your partner's solos that you might use in your future solos?		

Worksheet 10: Cookin' with the Rhythm Section

Full Name _____

	Good	Not So Good
Recording #1 Jazz Group with Soloist		
Recording #2 Jazz Group with Soloist		
Recording #3 Orff Group with Scat Singer		
Recording #4 Orff Group with Scat Singer		
Recording #5 My Class		

Worksheet 11: Jammin' on Sticky Situation

Full Name _____

Was our arrangement interesting to listen to? Why or why not?

Were the improvised solos interesting to listen to? Why or why not?

Did the solos and the rhythm section complement each other?

Did you find yourself listening to one instrument more than the others?
What was it and why do you think you focused on that part?

Was it cool?

Did it swing?

Worksheet 12: Compare Class Recording of
Sticky Situation to Jazz Group

Full Name _____

Two Versions of Sticky Situation

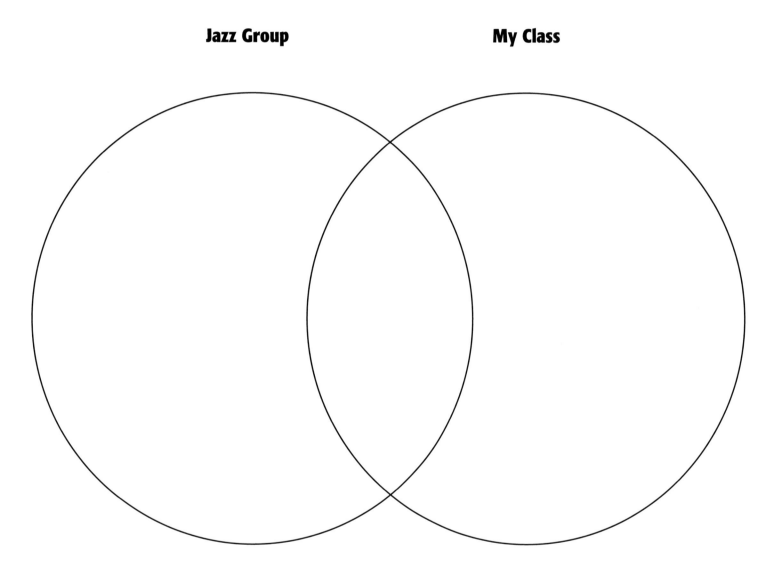

Jazz Group   **My Class**

Worksheet 13: Salt Peanuts Listening Map

Full Name _____

Salt Peanuts

Composed by John "Dizzy" Gillespie
Recorded by Dizzy Gillespie and His All Star Quintet

1.
2.
3.
4.
5.

6. THE TUNE
7. THE TUNE
8. THE TUNE WITH SINGING!

pea- "Salt nuts!" pea- "Salt nuts!"

Where given, circle the describing words that you think best fit the solo being played. Try to sing the salt peanuts part.

10. +

11. Honk! Honk!

9. loud lonely hyper
soft sad fast
boring
happy lots of notes
jumpy hip
cool
interesting slow

12.

13. sad
loud hip hyper
lonely boring
soft lots of notes
slow interesting
happy
fast funny cool jumpy
too many notes (PIANO SOLO)

14. cool
loud boring
soft interesting
slow low jumpy
fast high (SAX SOLO)

15. Trumpet and Sax "talk"

16. boring
soft high
slow interesting
loud
fast low jumpy
always the same
(TRUMPET SOLO)

17. hip boring
soft interesting
slow
fast jumpy
cool loud lots of sounds
dull (DRUM SOLO)

18.

19. SING! pea- "Salt nuts!" pea- "Salt nuts!"

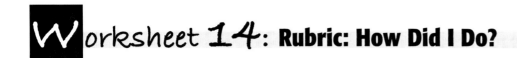

Full Name _____

Question	Fabulous!	OK	I Need to Woodshed

Woodshedding means "I need to practice, so I'll go out behind my house and practice in the woodshed where no one can hear until I come out as a Chop-Monster!"

Glossary & Basic Index of Musical Terms and Symbols

ACCENT > Play the note louder, with a special emphasis.

ACCIDENTAL ♭ ♯ ♮ A flat, sharp or natural sign that appears within a piece of music. An accidental sign affects the notes written on the same line or space following it for that measure only.

ACCOMPANIMENT Music that goes with or provides harmonic or rhythmic support for a melody.

ARRANGEMENT A version of a song that specifies when different instruments play, the groove and style, and where improvised solos occur.

ARTICULATION The manner in which a note is performed.

BAR LINE The lines which cross the staff and divide it into measures or bars.

BASS (or F) CLEF 𝄢 The clef used for notes in the lower pitch ranges.

BASS STAFF The staff on which the bass clef is placed. The two dots of the clef surround the line on which the note F is placed.

CALL-AND-RESPONSE A leader plays or sings a musical phrase (call) and a responder sings or plays an echo (response) or something different.

CAT A jazz musician (slang).

CHANGES A harmonic progression of chords, often called chord changes. The changes for a song often appear at the top of the melody on printed sheet music. A jazz rhythm section "comps" the changes when a musician plays a song melody or improvises. "Making the changes" means that a soloist improvises well, using notes that sound good with the changes.

CHOPS Great musical skills.

CHOP-MONSTER GROOVE Tapping two fingers into the palm of the opposite hand on beats 1 & 3 and clapping on beats 2 & 4.

CHOP-MONSTER MOVES Tapping waist for the root of major triad (chord), tapping shoulders for the third of a chord and tapping head for the fifth of the chord. With a minor triad, the third is flatted, so hug the shoulders for the third.

CHORD 3 or more notes sounding together.

CHORUS One time through the complete song form. Jazz musicians will often agree beforehand, or indicate while playing, how many choruses they will improvise to.

CLEF A sign that helps organize the staff so notes can be easily read.

COMP To accompany (slang). A jazz rhythm section comps chord changes behind melodies and improvised solos. Comping is an improvised art. For example pianists will use a song's chord progression as a basic guide and then add notes to the chords, play chords in different inversions or substitute with other complimentary chords.

CODA ⊕ An added ending.

D.C. (DA CAPO) Repeat from the beginning.

D.C. al CODA   Repeat from the beginning and play to ⊕, then skip to the ⊕ Coda.

D.C. al FINE   Repeat from the beginning and play to the end (Fine).

DOODLE-DAH   Rhythmic vocalization of a triplet.

DOT AFTER A NOTE ♩.   Increases the note's duration by half the original value.

DOTTED HALF NOTE ♩.   In $\frac{3}{4}$ and $\frac{4}{4}$ time signatures, it receives 3 beats.

DOTTED QUARTER NOTE ♩.   In time signatures with 4 as the bottom number, it receives 1½ beats.

DOUBLE BAR ‖   Is written at the end of a piece of music.

D.S. (DAL SEGNO)   Repeat from the sign 𝄋 .

D.S. al CODA   Repeat from the sign 𝄋 and play to ⊕, then skip to the ⊕ Coda.

D.S. al FINE   Repeat from the sign 𝄋 and play to the end (Fine).

DYNAMIC SIGNS   Indicate the volume, or how *soft* or *loud* the music should be played.

EIGHTH NOTE ♪ ♪♪   In time signatures with 4 as the bottom number, it receives ½ beat.

EIGHTH REST ♇   In time signatures with 4 as the bottom number, it receives ½ beat of silence.

FINE   The end.

1st and 2nd ENDINGS
Play or sing through the 1st ending to the repeat sign, then go back to the beginning.
When repeating, skip the 1st ending and play the 2nd.

FLAT ♭   Lowers the pitch by one half step.

GHOSTED NOTE   Hinting at a note but not playing or singing it loud enough to really hear it.

GRAND STAFF   The bass staff and treble staff connected by a brace and a line.

GROOVE   Rhythms fitting together in a good-sounding pattern.

HALF NOTE ♩   In time signatures with 4 as the bottom number, it receives 2 beats.

HALF REST ▬   In time signatures with 4 as the bottom number, it receives 2 beats of silence.

HI-HAT Two cymbals on a stand that the drummer plays with the foot, using a foot pedal.
When the pedal is pressed down with the foot the two cymbals come together and a sound is made.

HIP   Very cool and interesting. A musician can be hip, music can be hip and dancing can be hip.

IMPROVISER   A person who improvises a jazz solo.

IMPROVISATION   Extemporaneous creation of melody, within a given language, to the structure of a song.

INFLECTION Changing the sound of your voice. Using different pitches with different words.

JAM A musical workout, where jazz musicians gather to play for fun, and often improvise to challenging chord progressions. A jam session is not usually structured or planned in advance. Part of the fun is getting together with new musicians with new ideas.

JAZZ An American music coming out of West African and European influences. Improvisation is a key element of jazz. There are many styles of jazz including traditional, stride piano, swing, boogie-woogie, bebop, cool, hard bop, free and fusion.

KNEE-DLE DAH Pat right thigh, then left thigh, then clap. Knee-dle Dah goes with the Doo-dle Dah triplet rhythm.

LOCOMOTOR Movement that takes you to another place.

LEGATO To play or sing 2 or more notes smoothly connected.

MAJOR A key built upon a major scale, and based around the major chord, composed of notes 1, 3 & 5 of the scale.

MEASURE (or **BAR**) The area between two bar lines.

MIDDLE C The note in the middle of the grand staff and the C nearest the middle of the keyboard

MINOR A key built upon a minor scale, and based upon the minor chord, composed of notes 1, 3 & 5 of the scale.

NATURAL SIGN ♮ The natural sign before a note cancels a previous flat or sharp.

NOTES o ♩ ♩ ♪ The oval-shaped symbols that are placed on the lines and in the spaces of the staff. They represent musical sounds called pitches.

MONSTER An exceptionally talented jazz musician.

NON-LOCOMOTOR Movement that stays in one place.

PASTCHEN or PATSCH A thigh slap.

PITCH A musical sound.

QUARTER NOTE ♩ In time signatures with 4 as the bottom number, it receives 1 beat.

QUARTER REST ❩ In time signatures with 4 as the bottom number, it receives 1 beat of silence.

REPEAT SIGN :‖ Return to the beginning or previous repeat sign ‖: at the beginning of the section.

RHYTHM Combinations of sound and rests.

RHYTHM SECTION A group of instruments that may include piano (keyboard), bass, guitar and drums. The rhythm section makes clear the harmonic structure of the groove.

RIDE CYMBAL A suspended cymbal on a stand that allows the cymbal to "ride." Ride cymbals are played with drum sticks.

RIFF Short, repeated musical phrase used as a background for a soloist, or as an improvised idea.

RUBRIC A set of descriptors used to make assessment more uniform.

SCAT Vocal technique that uses horn-like syllables to improvise solos.

SHARP ♯ Raises the pitch by one half step.

SLUR Smoothly connects two or more notes of different pitches by a curved line over or under the notes.

SOLO Improvised melody played or sung by one person.

STACCATO ♩ Play the note short and detached.

STAFF The five lines and the fourspaces between them on which music notes and other symbols are written.

STEADY BEAT The underlying pulse present in most music that stays steady throughout a song.

SWING The basic rhythmic feel of jazz in which the rhythm section is responsible for providing a feeling of being propelled forward. Swing is a defining characteristic of jazz. It is also a style of jazz that first appeared in the 1930s featuring big bands playing arrangements for dancing.

SWING EIGHTH NOTES A performance practice in which the first of two eighth notes receives approximately ⅔ of the value of that beat, while the 2nd of the two is more often accented or articulated.

TEMPO A word meaning "rate of speed". It tells how fast or slow to play the music.

TIE Two notes of the same pitch joined by a curved line over or under the note. Each note joined by a tie is held for its full value but only the first note is played or sung.

TIME SIGNATURE $\frac{4}{4}\frac{3}{4}\frac{2}{4}$ Appears at the beginning of the music after the clef sign. It contains two numbers.
The upper number tells how many beats are in each measure; the lower number indicates what type of note receives 1 beat.

TRADE FOURS Alternating 4-measure improvised solos with one or more musicians.

TREBLE (or G) **CLEF** The clef used for notes in the higher pitch ranges.

TREBLE STAFF The staff on which the treble clef is placed.
The curl of the clef circles the line on which the note G is placed.

TRIPLET FEEL The underlying doo-dle dah feel in swing.

VENN DIAGRAM Two large, overlapping circles that are used to show concepts that are in common (within the overlap) and concepts that are unique to each circle (written inside the part of the circle not overlapping).

WALKING BASS A steady bass line, often at a walking tempo, characterized by stepwise passing tones that connect chord roots and chord tones.

WHOLE NOTE 𝅝 In time signatures with 4 as the bottom number, it receives 4 beats.

WHOLE REST ▬ Means to rest for a whole measure. In $\frac{3}{4}$ it receives 3 beats; in $\frac{4}{4}$ it receives 4 beats; in $\frac{2}{4}$ it receives 2 beats.

About the Authors

Margaret Fitzgerald

Margaret Fitzgerald is a General Music and Instrumental Teacher with the Brookfield, Connecticut Public Schools. She has been teaching for 25 years in various rooms, closets and hallways. Margaret holds BS and MS degrees in Music Education from WCSU and a 6th year degree in administration from SCSU, both in Connecticut. She has been published in several MENC publications, and is on the Executive Board for the Connecticut Music Educators Association (CMEA). Fitzgerald and McCord were the recipients of the Apple Education Innovation Grant as well as the Computer World/ Smithsonian Award in 1999. Margaret has been Teacher of the Year for her school, the town of Brookfield and was CMEA Elementary Music Educator of the Year in 2000. She has presented workshops for MENC, IAJE, BOCES and CMEA. Margaret resides in New Milford, Connecticut with her husband, Mike, and their three sons, Matthew, Benjamin and Andrew. She enjoys playing French horn (along with her husband on trombone) in the Candlewood Brass Quintet. E-mail: mfitzmusic@aol.com

Shelly Berg

Shelly Berg is Professor of Music and former Chair of Jazz Studies in the Thornton School of Music at the University of Southern California. The Los Angeles Times calls him "a powerhouse jazz pianist who always swings hard." His CD *The Will* (CARS Records) spent eight weeks in the Top Ten of the U.S. Jazz Radio Charts (Gavin). Dave Brubeck raves, "Shelly Berg is a great jazz pianist who has a total command of his instrument." A past president of the International Association for Jazz Education (IAJE), Shelly was the recipient of the 2002 IAJE Lawrence Berk Leadership Award and the Los Angeles Jazz Society 2003 Educator of the Year Award.

He has appeared as a lecturer, performer, or all-state guest clinician throughout the United States as well as in Canada, Mexico, Europe, Japan and Israel. He has numerous compositions for jazz ensemble in publication, and is the author of the *Chop-Monster* improvisation series (Alfred Publishing) and *Jazz Improvisation: The Goal-Note Method* (Kendor Music). Shelly has orchestrated for Kiss, Chicago, and Richard Marx and his film orchestration credits include Warner Bros. *Almost Heroes* and *Three to Tango*, Fox's *Men of Honor* and the NBC mini-series *The '60s*. His orchestrations are called "magnificent. . . incredible" by Johnny Mandel. E-mail: SheltBerg@aol.com

Kimberly McCord

Kimberly McCord is Assistant Professor and Coordinator for Undergraduate Music Education at Illinois State University. She teaches elementary and secondary general music methods along with graduate music education courses. She holds a DME and MME from the University of Northern Colorado and a BM from the University of Nebraska at Omaha. Previously she taught instrumental and general music for ten years in the Denver Public Schools. She is a frequent presenter at national, regional and state MENC conferences, the International Association for Jazz Education (IAJE), International Society for Music Education (ISME) and many others. She is on the IAJE Resource Team for general music and has presented at IAJE summer Teacher Training Institutes. Her publications include *Strategies for Teaching Technology* (MENC) and she has contributed articles to a variety of music education and jazz journals. E-mail: KimJazz@aol.com